AF615869

SUCCESS SUTRAS FOR THE 21ST CENTURY : A TRILOGY OF WISDOM

- ☐ Chanakya's Political Wisdom
- ☐ Confucius' Social Wisdom
- ☑ Kabir's Spiritual Wisdom

Presenting

Kabir's Spiritual Wisdom

SUCCESS SUTRAS FOR THE 21ST CENTURY : A TRILOGY OF WISDOM

- ☐ **Chanakya's Political Wisdom**
- ☐ **Confucius' Social Wisdom**
- ☑ **Kabir's Spiritual Wisdom**

VIVEKACHARYA PAVAN CHOUDARY

Wisdom Guru

&

Author of the world acclaimed book -

When You Are Sinking Become a Submarine

A WVPD ORIGINAL

Books from Wisdom Village (Publications Division) envision to enhance and enrich its readers with life changing experiences from the mind, body and soul genres. They strive towards holistic development.

Editorial Coordinator	Charushilla Narula
Design	Arpan Advertising & Marketing

First published 2009

 This book is part of the three books in the Trilogy of Wisdom by Vivekacharya Pavan Choudary.

ISBN 978-81-906555-4-5

Published by:

Wisdom Village (Publications Division)
Knowledge is information. Wisdom is transformation.

WVPD is a part of Wisdom Village
124 Satya Niketan
IInd Floor,
New Delhi - 110021
Email: wisdomvillageindia@gmail.com
Contact Person: Charushilla Narula

CONTENTS

ABOUT VIVEKACHARYA PAVAN CHOUDARY

Vivekacharya Pavan Choudary is a world icon in Success Coaching, Political thinking & Practical Spirituality. He has been acknowledged for his global contributions in the fields of Wisdom, Leadership, Management, Psychology, Creativity, State Craft & Spirituality. Today he is among the foremost thinkers of the world in breadth and depth of thinking. By sharing his ideas and insights he has contributed to the success of sportstars, film stars, CEOs and the political elite both in India and abroad. So pioneering are his thoughts that they have initiated a wave of social reform, which is gradually adding to the national fabric.

His world acclaimed book, 'When You Are Sinking Become a Submarine', expounds a new philosophy of power and success. It has crossed Indian shores and is becoming a reference text for leaders worldwide. It has already been translated in Hindi (Aisa Paal Taane ki Aandhi Urja Bane) and editions in other languages are soon to be launched.

A leader, on the path of nation building Vivekacharya has moved from strength to strength and today he is being viewed as the most promising political thinker and management speaker, shaping opinions on practically all aspects of governance, social reform and leadership. Not a pundit but a successful practitioner, Vivekacharya Pavan Choudary, is the CEO and MD of Vygon, a leading French Multinational in the field of Healthcare.

Considering his unmatched profile and the quality of his research in the fields of socio-politico-spiritual wisdom, it was only apt for WVPD to request him to compile this unique **Trilogy of Wisdom**, a path-breaking commentary on Chanakya's Political Wisdom, Confucius' Social Wisdom and Kabir's Spiritual Wisdom.

For more details on the author and to order other titles please visit www.starcoach.co.in

A NOTE FROM THE PUBLISHER

Wisdom Village (Publications Division) (WVPD) proudly presents SUCCESS SUTRAS FOR THE 21ST CENTURY: A TRILOGY OF WISDOM By VIVEKACHARYA PAVAN CHOUDARY. This is a unique rendition (in print and audio) of **Chanakya's Political Wisdom, Confucius' Social Wisdom and Kabir's Spiritual Wisdom as has never been presented before.** It is an attempt to make the wisdom of these great masters relevant to us today.

Vivekacharya Pavan Choudary, in this epic-like trilogy, accompanied with its soul-stirring audio version, provides a ready guide to achieving Political sharpness, Social order and Spiritual bliss.

KABIR & VIVEKACHARYA

Vivekacharya Pavan Choudary believes that the spiritual quest and human desires can coexist. The scenario in India is such that so much energy has been wasted on airy-fairy, hocus pocus spiritual recreation that it has only made us impotent as a nation. Religion has been hyped, abused and used as the remote to charge and aggravate people. In the end, some people have solved their hidden agendas (namely politicians or Gurus) and the others have been left looking like buffoons, mindless followers. At such a time, Vivekacharya shares the importance of imbibing Kabir and his teachings for self realisation.

According to Vivekacharya, Kabir, through his dohas has presented a guide to good and wise living, of how one can connect with the spiritual, achieve the material and make every stage of life more meaningful and fulfilling. What Kabir wrote many hundreds of years ago is uncannily relevant today. Vivekacharya highlights how some of his writings are 'radical truths.' **The realisation of these *radical truths is the key to enlightenment.***

Welcome to your first true understanding of Spirituality as the Sutra for Success.

Charushilla Narula
wisdomvillageindia@gmail.com

INTRODUCTION

Saint Kabir has been one of the most unique Indian poet thinkers. Achieving a peak in spiritual consciousness, Kabir was not just a spiritual guru. Kabir's dohas or couplets have been widely translated and attempts to interpret them have also been made. However, most of this interpretation is esoteric and academic. It often does not do justice to this great master of his times.

The following pages truly highlight the essence of Kabir, not as a poet or spiritualist alone, but as a Success Guru. Vivekacharya Pavan Choudary, in this inimitable compilation, is making Kabir address issues of mentoring, love, friendship, humility, courage, desire, success, greed, speech, wisdom and many others - that present themselves before us. One often wonders if Kabir knew of the dilemmas of the 21st century or have the predicaments of life been the same always.

Is enlightenment an illusion?
What is self realisation?
What defines a spiritual person?
Can spirituality and material success coexist?
How can one create enduring bases to success?

As the commentary to follow addresses the above questions, many more questions get answered along the way. Guiding you towards successful pursuits through spiritual indoctrination, you are about to witness as never before, a trance into self realisation and achievement through Kabir.

Spiritual Wisdom of Kabir

Kabir is a man of candor. He has spoken extensively on the guru-shishya (teacher-student) relationship. Let us begin this book by looking at the teacher-student relationship in the first few *dohas* (couplets). In the whole world, I doubt if anyone has written so extensively on the teacher-student relationship as Kabir has. He shares rather openly, what according to him, is detrimental to the exchange of knowledge. Being a man of candor, he realises, just as anyone in an organization would, that candor reduces the time spent on a job. Candor also saves money. And most importantly, Kabir realises that candor draws people into a discussion through which people get idea rich. And in this *doha,* he really draws you into contemplation, you almost get into a dialogue with Kabir.

आगे अंधा कूप में, दूजा लिया बुलाय ।
दोनो डूबे बापुरे, निकसे कौन उपाय ।।

Kabir cautions of a Guru who is himself in delusion.
Such a Guru is already drowned in darkness and
worsens the situation of his confused disciple.

Let us try and understand what Kabir says in this couplet. He frankly expresses his opinion about a poor teacher. This couplet is about a guru, a teacher, who doesn't know. It is a fact that there are many gurus in the world who themselves do not know. They have reached that position / pulpit and are disseminating knowledge just to serve their egos. If you take advice / teaching from such a stereotype personality then you are bound to lose. For instance, if you ask for counsel, from a person who thinks aggression is the panacea to all ills, he would advise you to be aggressive only. That is the only remedy he has. Abraham Maslow has said, *When the only tool you own is a hammer, every problem begins to resemble a nail.*

So in this couplet, Kabir is cautioning you. Before selecting a guide, ensure that he is not a stereotype personality. Ensure that he is not an ignoramus, who thinks he knows. The guru chosen, should be wise and balanced. He should not be someone who projects his own frustrations or his own ignorance on his students. He should not be someone whose paranoia or lopsided views rub off on them and they also start sharpening the spoons in their kitchen into knives. He is asking the students to choose their guru wisely. If the guru is blind and is followed by a blind student, then (in one of his *dohas* Kabir has said, *Andha Andha theliyen*) how can a blind man lead another blind man.

जौन मिला सो गुरू मिला, चेला मिला न कोय ।
चेला को चेला मिलै, तब कछु होय तो होय ।।

Kabir says that the world is full of egoists and Gurus.
Very few realise that a true guru or mentor is a disciple first.
True knowledge exchange is possible only when one understands this fact.

In this couplet, Kabir says that the world is full of egoist gurus. Very few realise that a true guru is one who is a disciple also; the quest / thirst for knowledge is so deep in him, that he always moves with the metaphorical school-bag on his shoulder. Such gurus are rare. Most gurus know or have a lopsided view of reality.

In India, there exists the guru-shishya parampara (teacher-student tradition), which invokes the student to behave in a particular way with the teacher. This tradition tells the student that he should be respectful and highly obedient to his guru. The purpose of the tradition was to orient the student so that he could learn from the guru. But we are very smart people. We looked at the tradition and thought to ourselves that the guru gets so many advantages in this relationship. He is in a really comfortable and enviable position. So then why become a student, let's become a guru only. And so everybody in India wants to become a Guru.

I had a peon in my office who was about 60 years of age. His name was Phool Singh. He was a very ordinary peon. His caliber was ordinary and his work ethics were also nothing to write home about. But we kept him, as we knew that he would be retiring shortly. And every time there was a religious ceremony in the office, whether Diwali or Holi, because he was the eldest, we allowed him to offer prayers, standing in the centre with the *Aarti thali* (a plate carrying condiments and offerings for invocation to the Lord). At such occasions, I used to stand on his right and my Head of Sales, on his left. Soon he retired and went to his village. Recently, when I was approaching my office, I saw a bearded man at my door step. He greeted me, I greeted him back respectfully. And then I heard him say, "Sir, have you not recognised me?" I peered closely only to find that it was our Phool Singh! So I asked him about his attire, "What's all this Phool Singh? Why are you donning orange clothes and a beard?" He said, "I have become a guru Sir."

So I said, "Ok. So you have become a guru in your village in Uttar Pradesh?" He said, "No Sir. I did go there and I wanted to become a guru there, but there were already so many gurus Sir, who did not want their monopoly to be upset. They had formed a cartel and they told me that I could not practise there. So I went to Bastar (a region near Raipur in Chattisgarh, one of the Central states of India). I have settled down there. Now everybody in and around the village knows me."

"That's very good." I said.

"Sir, they know you also." He said.

And I felt, Wow! My word has reached the remote corners of Bastar. From Boston to Bastar, my word was reaching everywhere and I felt very good.

"How is it that they know me?" I asked.

He took out a file and on one side of the file there were pasted several clippings of newspapers with my picture with some captions saying 'Pavan Choudary in town'. These were about six months to a year old, when a newspaper called Dainik Bhaskar had invited me to Chattisgarh and then provided the publicity. Looking at those clippings, I felt that he was like my ambassador telling about me to everybody. Only until I looked at the other side of the file where I saw that there was a big Diwali picture, where he was standing in front of the Goddess Lakshmi offering prayers and I stood on his right and my Head of Sales on his left. Now I understood what he must have been telling everyone "This is the teacher / guru (who is being talked about in the clippings). He used to be my right hand man when I was in service and was my student."

I was intrigued and I almost felt how ingenious he was to improve his credentials so. Also as he was a bit of a wishy-washy or slippery kind of person even when he was in my office so I wasn't surprised by what he was doing.

So I asked him, "What kinds of questions are asked of you?"

"All kinds of questions are asked and I answer them absolutely perfectly."

"Give me an example."

"Some people ask me, where does God live. So I tell them, He lives in *Kshir Sagar*[*]. I tell them that there is a lotus popping out of his navel. He is lying on a bed of roses."

So sure he was that this is where God lived.

Who has taught Phool Singh?

Another such guru has taught him.

A guru who has no understanding of God or godliness. Many such people are propagating things that they do not know or things they have not experienced.

[*]*Kshir Sagar is the name of a mythological sea.*

They are propagating them to every willing listener. And this is the issue that Kabir is trying to attack. Kabir says that first be a student and then be a teacher and even when you are a teacher, stay a student. Keep learning. As long as this metaphorical school bag, I mentioned before, is on your shoulders, you will keep learning, you will keep young and one day you can even qualify to be a real guru. Guru in Hindi means, the one who makes darkness disappear, the one who lights your path. You will become a true guru only when you become a true student.

गुरू बिचारा क्या करै, शब्द न लागा अंग ।
कहैं कबीर मैली गजी, कैसे लागै रंग ।।

Kabir laments that if a disciple is not a worthy person, then a Guru cannot do much to his already existing state of ignorance. It is like trying to dye / colour a dirty bed sheet that will never catch the colour.

Kabir means that the fragrant winds coming from the sandalwood trees do not aromate the bamboo groves that continue to be offensive smelling. If the owl cannot see during the day, is the sun to be blamed?

Ignorance is not an empty slate. It is usually a slate on which much has been written. It is a slate on which so much has been written that there is no space to write anymore. It is a slate which has been written upon with an indelible chalk. So it is easy to train an innocent mind, but it is difficult to train the half-baked scholar. This is what Kabir is trying to say, it is like trying to dye a dirty bed sheet that will never catch the colour. Why would a half-baked scholar pose resistance to learning? Because unknowingly, he judges as he is listening. He evaluates what he hears through his rusted calipers, attributes meaning where there isn't any, and misinterprets attributes the wrong meaning. His existing state of half-baked knowledge does not allow the guru to work on him.

This is the problem that Kabir is referring to in this couplet. Just as the fragrant winds coming from the sandalwood trees do not aromate the bamboo groves that continue to be offensive smelling, it is difficult to train a student who is burdened with such ignorance. The teacher cannot do anything in such a state. The student, because of his half-baked knowledge is closed to learning.

जब मैं था तब गुरू नहीं, अब गुरू है मैं नाहिं ।
प्रेम गली अति सांकरी, तामें दो न समाहिं ।।

Kabir says that when in a state of ego
a disciple cannot connect to his Guru.
And when he does achieve that connection with the Guru
and absorbs true knowledge, ego vanishes.
So narrow is the lane of love between the Guru and disciple
that it has no room for ego.

Ego has its uses and Kabir knows about them. Ego is a defense mechanism. It helps you defend your interest. However, one should use ego as a rain coat. Only when there is rain, do you use a raincoat. It is not part of your daily attire, you don't wear it all the time. If you were to wear it everyday or all the time, then you would be uncomfortable. You would also make others around you very uncomfortable.

In this verse, Kabir says that ego is of no use in the classroom. But how is ego born in a student ? The first reason for the birth of ego in the student is exploitation by the teacher. Many a teacher has exploited the student by asking him to drop his ego, by asking him to obey blindly. Infact, history is full of teachers like these. And in such a case, ego surfaces in a student to defend his own self-interest. The other, more important reason for the birth of ego is because of all the egalitarian talk happening in the West and coming to the East. As the world has become a global village whatever is uttered in the West, almost simultaneously reaches the East. And cultures are porous to this influence.

When Alexander came to India, he found that in India the king is treated like a God. So he declared himself a king. In the West, when Aristotle's nephew protested against this declaration and said that he did not accept Alexander's God-hood, Alexander had him executed. Then, when Aristotle, who had coached Alexander, went to him and told him that he had made a grievous error by executing his nephew, Alexander said, "Even philosophers are not immune to my wrath." He was telling Aristotle that in case he also did not accept his God-hood, he would not hesitate in executing his teacher as well. Such was Aristotle's Eastern influence on the West. This was the time when the East was culturally and socially, far ahead of the West. Today we have the western influence on the East. The people in the West, rather the ignorant people in the West are saying that all men are equal. They are talking about egalitarianism and this is even reaching the ears of the students. It has become another reason for the birth of ego in the students.

Through the birth of the student's ego, the sacred space between the teacher and the student gets violated. Kabir knows of this 'sacred space'. He knows that this sacred space is critical to learning. In its absence, no learning will happen. Kabir's point has been validated by Freud also. Freud also speaks of the sacred space between the teacher and the student without which, exchange of learning does not happen. I wouldn't say that Freud visited India or that he learnt it from Kabir (It is very fashionable among us Indians that whenever we hear something which resembles what our great men have said by someone else in the West, we immediately try to bring a teacher-student connection there). The books that I have read do not say that Freud visited India, but Freud was a peak in consciousness, as was Kabir. And as it often happens, two great men, thousands of miles away from each other or separated by hundreds of years, think of the same thing.

For that matter, Buddha also knew that a space of respect needs to be present between the teacher and the student. Only then can the teacher share his learnings with the student. There is an episode in Buddha's life, before his enlightenment. As he gets enlightened, he goes to a woman who is an *untouchable** and accepts coconut rice from her and eats to his heart's content. He has five disciples then, who see him doing this. At that time, Buddha was advocating complete abstinence and penance. He was advocating living on just one grain of rice a day. And these disciples now see him eating to his heart's content and moreover, eating from a woman's hand and that too an untouchable woman. They feel the master has been corrupted. They don't understand that enlightenment has taught him that all these things don't matter. What you eat, through whose hands you eat, are of no consequence and in no way connected to enlightenment. The master had realised that penance is not the door to enlightenment. But the students were judging him by the standards that he had set for himself as well as for them. So these five students desert Buddha. Once Buddha realises this, he goes looking for them. And he finds them sitting at a river bank. As he is approaching them, among each other, they decide not to give him any respect. They decide to address him as *Gautam*** and not as the enlightened one. So when Buddha approaches them, they behave

**Untouchable = from the lowest caste.*

***Gautam was Buddha's first name.*

disdainfully with him and also address him as Gautam. This is when Buddha says, "I have discovered the truth and I want to share it with you. If you would disrespect me and call me Gautam, somewhere at the back of my mind, I will be uncomfortable, my sharing will not be spontaneous, and you might miss me. So continue to behave with me just as you did earlier and continue to listen to me." Buddha is re-establishing the 'sacred space' necessary between a teacher and a student for exchange of knowledge to happen.

This space has been recognised by Buddha, by Kabir, by Freud and now even by Sarkozy. Nicolas Sarkozy (President of France) also spoke of the same space when he in his election manifesto said that he would make the students address the teachers as Wu not Tu. (In Hindi, Aap is the equivalent of the French, Wu and Tu of Tu). Essentially, he says, that teachers will be addressed more respectfully by the students. That means that he understands this over egalitarian approach is leading to chaos. People are becoming less educated rather than more educated. They are more aware about their rights but they are completely ignorant about the truth because they are not willing to give to the teacher the space to teach them. The same truth has been acknowledged by L. Porter, one of the leading lights in the fields of education. His research says, the good students appreciate discipline, because discipline enables an environment in which they can learn. The bad / trouble-making students also appreciate discipline. This finding shakes or challenges the 1990s belief in laissez-faire, that spoke of giving the child his complete and unbridled freedom reflected in the song,

We don't need no education, we don't need no thought control,
no dark sarcasm in the classroom, teacher leave the kids alone.

If the guru is a good guru, the student will realise that he has much to gain. If the student is worthy and respectful, the guru gains confidence in the future of their relationship. He also gains comfort in sharing what he knows and what he feels is very important for the student to know. Ego from both ends starts vanishing. The student and the teacher start fusing or becoming one. They start becoming one family or the best of friends who guard each others interest, who have each other's genuine interest in their hearts. They become one. This is what Kabir means when he says, *Prem gali ati sakri, jaame do na samaye,* that is, their identities start fusing and they become unaware of the fact that they are two people. They start thinking, feeling, and operating like one unit.

भय बिन भाव न ऊपजै, भय बिनु होय न प्रीति ।
जब हिरदे से भय गया, मिटी सकल रस रीति ।।

Kabir says that without an element of fear,
it is difficult to feel happinessor sorrow.
Fear is important even to feel affection for the Guru.
In the absence of fear, one loses reverence for his master and
can easily abandon all ethical behaviour,
resulting in a loss of his own identity.

Every mother, once in a while, has to scare her child. Why? Does she not love her child? No. If there is one expression of love, it is the love between the mother and the child. She loves her child, almost as she loves herself, and sometimes even more. Ever wondered how easy it is to please a mother? You just have to say, “Mom, I'm hungry.” - This is enough to galvanize her into action. And she is on an ecstatic trip now. She is making / cooking something for her child. And while you might think it is labour, it is only a labour of love for her. And that is the kind of love she has for her child. Then, why does she scare the child once in a while. Two reasons Sometimes there is an urgency of result which is required. Maybe she has to board a train and the child is not letting go. So the mother says, “Let me go now or the policeman will catch you.” Or sometimes, the child, because of his lack of knowledge and understanding, is about to harm himself or another, which is when the mother uses a scare tactic. Now even when she uses this tactic and the child responds negatively by crying against it, somewhere at the back of the child's mind, he understands that what the mother is doing is in his best interest. So, the mother in many ways preserves the child. With time, this bond of love between the mother and the child is able to grow with the understanding that discipline is important.

By fear, Kabir refers to discipline. For him discipline is a type of love only. It is a tough love. But the quality of fear generated should be good. That is, the person being disciplined must understand that this discipline is for his long term good. It is not to harass him or not to give him what is his due. It is for his good. It is this kind of fear that Kabir talks of in this couplet. He feels that without this kind of fear, often love can't be born, and if born, love will not flourish if such a fear is completely absent.

Also fear serves as the backdrop for love. For love to stand out, you need a background. In order to think of yourself as a man of love, you will have to give up the idea of thinking of yourself as a man who never goes to war. History has called upon men for such decisions. This is true in most individual and personal relationships. Life may, more than once, call upon you to prove who you are by demonstrating an aspect of who you are not. Have you ever wondered why Jesus Christ, a true man of love, chased out the money-changers with a whip? Perhaps, because he knew that love wouldn't work there. Or he felt that the time for love was up. It was time for discipline. This kind of discipline accentuates the image of love. It becomes the right background through which love stands out and is not taken for granted. This is another way in which fear or discipline makes love more prominent, more noticeable, more worthy.

However, a good guru knows when to use love and when to use fear. Imagine, a peon in my office comes to me and says that he needs some money to buy books for his son and if he can get a loan for that. I have a few thousand rupees in my pocket and I willingly give it to him and I know I'm never going to ask him to give it back. Next day, another peon comes with a similar request and I tell him to manage his finances better, he would get nothing from me and I ask him to go away. He leaves with moist eyes, dejected and disappointed. But I am at peace because I know that this peon is a drunkard. He is careless with his money and not responsible in his duty towards the organization or towards his family, so I send him away and my inner voice does not protest. If I had similarly sent the first peon away, who was a responsible, dedicated employee, then my inner voice would have protested. It would have asked *what you are doing. This is not the way to behave with this man*. So you have to train your inner voice to speak. And you have to learn to listen to this inner voice. If you can do that then depending on the need of the situation, you know when you require love and when you need to be tough.

This is another couplet full of Kabir's candor. Very few people have been able to express things so candidly. In this book we have tried to study and comment on those couplets which are not hyperbolic. They are true, practical and carry the eternal essence of life in them.

झूठा सब संसार है, कोउ न अपना मीत ।
राम नाम को जानि ले, चलै सो भौजल जीत ।।

Kabir says that this world of knavery, guile and attraction is false.
There is no one here who can be called a true friend.
Everyone is selfish.
Therefore wisdom lies in dedicating yourself
to the quest of knowing the all pervasive Creator,
for only he can free you from the bindings of this ocean-like world.

Kabir looks at the world as it is. He looks at the world with an X-ray vision. He says that this is a world of knavery, of guile and falsehood. He peeps beneath the noble utterances of people and finds selfish motives. He expresses that no one here can be called a true friend, everyone is selfish and all relationships are utilitarian. Even a wife has to look good or be an earning member or provide services to maintain utility. For that matter, everyone has to maintain utility for others. As long as this utility is there, a person is wanted and respected by others. Once this utility is not there, very few in the world do their duty towards you. Some family members may do their duty towards you but they too stay gripped, from time to time, with the thought that you are not pulling your burden yourself.

In this verse, this is the point that Kabir is highlighting. He says that it is better for you to try and remember the Lord or try to connect with the universal essence. Only then you can be free from the ties of this world, most of which are false. When you go in search of the universal essence, that search occupies you and then these false relationships do not engage much of your time or energy. The search becomes your raison d'etre - the reason for your being.

भय से भक्ति करै सबै, भय से पूजा होय ।
भय पारस है जीव को, निर्भय होय न कोय ।।

Kabir philosophises that 'fear' (probably of the unknown) is instrumental in moving people towards prayer and taking to devotional practices. Fear works like the philosopher's stone that causes people to tread on the right path.

Kabir reaches the heart of the matter. He says, fear is instrumental in moving people towards prayer and taking to devotional practices.

How was prayer or religion born?

Imagine the time of the Paleolithic man. Why did he fold his hands in prayer? Possibly, at that time lightning, floods, other calamities and death - were not explainable. So, the sky which was blazing and the thunders which were rumbling made him kneel out of apprehension and he started praying. And God, as we know, was born in the mind of man.

Then, as society progressed, some people made a fence around a piece of land and started calling it their own. They marked a boundary and somehow made other people accept it. All powerful people marked a boundary and the concept of private property came into existence.

Another emotion followed - Greed. If you didn't have property you were considered a failure. So greed was also, in the beginning, linked to failure (fear of failure). It was the fear of failure which fanned the greedy instinct in man. Man started thinking that if he does not have property then he will be considered a failure, he won't be able to do much and would be deserted by even by his near and dear ones. So man started bowing down to God; not only to protect himself but also to progress materially. So this prayer and devotion was born basically out of fear. Fear was the original source, the fountain head. Now, Kabir is not belittling the man who has begun worshiping because of fear. Kabir feels that it doesn't matter what brings you close to God; if it is fear, so be it. The important thing is that you come close to God. The trigger is not important. The outcome is.

Fear also works like the philosopher's stone that causes people to tread on the right path. Most people also take to religion because of fear. They morally discipline themselves because of fear. Hence, fear is a stepping stone to spirituality. Your thoughts, words, deeds and relationships start changing because you take to prayer. Slowly, a new connection is born between you and let's say, God. Earlier, you were bowing to him only because of fear and then slowly, because you change, another relationship with this universal spirit starts forming. This means, prayer helps you align yourself better with that force field of goodness (let us call it) God. First it aligns you better, then it conditions you and as this conditioning is happening, slowly fear starts disappearing. You stop thinking that God is a capricious personality who is only there to keep account of your sins and virtues and maintain a balance sheet or he is someone who has to, from time to time, punish you for all your wrong doings.

So Kabir says that the first step towards religion is taken because of fear. Therefore, fear not only initiates your relationship with God, fear takes you to the platform where there is a possibility of change in this relationship.

And in this verse, Kabir highlights this utility of fear - How fear transforms a man and how it is the scaffolding on which the spiritual edifice is erected.

पाप पुण्य की संका नहिं, स्वर्ग नरक नहिं जाहिं ।
कहत कबीर सुनहुरे संतो, जहां का तहां समाहिं ।।

Kabir says that he has no concern for piety or sin, heaven or hell. He believes that steadiness of mind can be attained wherever you are and self-knowledge is what takes you far.

Kabir has risen over piety or sin. He understands that virtue and sin in the religious domain are artificial constructs and so are heaven and hell. He has risen above these. He believes that for steadiness of mind you don't have to go anywhere. Peace does not dwell in the temple. In fact, more than peace, politics dwells in the temple. And Kabir understands this. He knows that rather than your pious behaviour, it is self knowledge which will take you far.

In the Roman language, the equivalent of the word 'perfect' means 'to be complete' and a person can't be complete without an evil part. Knowing that you have an evil part and knowing how to keep it in check, that is being perfect and that will free you. It will let you accept your humanity, see what you are and help you attain self-knowledge. This self-knowledge will take you far. One must understand that the artificial constructs of heaven and hell will only limit your growth.

भगति दुहेली राम की, जैसी खांड़े की धार ।
जो डोले तो कटि पड़े, नहि तो उतरे पार ।।

Kabir says that treading the path of devotion
is nothing short of walking on a sharp razor.
The slightest of faltering can get you severely cut.
However, if you move with caution and stay steady,
you attain that inner state of bliss / salvation.

Here Kabir talks about the path of *Bhakti* (devotion). He says that the path of devotion is nothing short of walking on a sharp razor. The slightest of faltering can get you severely cut.

He means that when you are on this Bhakti path you should be supremely poised, because this path can take you to mysticism and if you become a mystic you have to somehow incorporate your mystical knowledge into your overall understanding of things. It is as if you are swimming in the ocean towards the horizon where the waterline meets the skyline, and you see a supernal light at the horizon, a lovely fascinating light. Imagine that this is the mystic light. You become so fascinated with this mystic light that you stop moving your arms and legs as you are supposed to, for keeping afloat; you will surely start drowning. So mysticism should not so fascinate you that you start drowning or failing in day to day life. Know that the path of Bhakti taken to the extreme can make you an incorrigible mystic. Kabir is one of the few who understands this side-effect of Bhakti. That's why he urges you to be supremely poised. You should not fail in your day to day life just because you are seeing the mystic light. Watch it, yet escape drowning. Bring that balance.

Kabir also knows that the path of devotion can take you into rituals and even superstitions. You can start imagining a reality which is getting constructed only because of your passion. This is the other reason why he says that when you are on this path of devotion be extremely careful. Be balanced.

This balance will take you to bliss. This balance will take you to salvation, to beatitude to *Sachidanand* (supreme spiritual pleasure).

तेरे अन्दर सांच जो, बाहर नाहिं जनाव ।
जानन हारा जानि है, अन्तर गति का भाव ।।

Kabir condemns bragging even about the truth in your heart.
Your truth is yours alone.
The knowledgeable have the ability to
sense the machinations of the human mind on their own and
your true heart will be seen by them anyways.

Why do we brag about our spiritual realisations?
Why do we want to tell others about our spiritual growth?
There are two reasons for this.
Either it is for one-up-man-ship: somewhere we want the other to know that not only you but I am also spiritual and maybe, more spiritual. Such kind of a competition is very prevalent in India. We cannot tolerate the fact that God is bestowing his mercies and revealing his essence to our neighbour and not to us. Which is why, whenever the conversation drifts towards such issues every Indian comes up with his own realisations. And now, the West is also catching this virus.

The other reason, why we talk about our spiritual realisations is more subtle. We use the talk of our spiritual realisations to ensnare other people, to attract them to us. These are label talks. They label us. They are meant to tell the other person that *you must really be very virtuous and that is why God is so close to you and which is why you are having all these realisations*. So we set up our candidature through such talk.

But Kabir knows that the gains from either of this (through one-up-man-ship or attracting people through your spiritual realisations) are far lower than the cost of doing so. Because post verbalizing there are two realities that present themselves - one is, what you realised and the other is, what you have spoken. Now because you cannot exactly translate what you have realised, into words, the words lose their essence. This is because the realisation is very fluid or gossamer fine and words are very concrete. When translated into words much is lost in the translation. The authenticity of the spiritual realisation now is under attack by its description. Now it will be difficult for you to feel that spiritual reality with the same intensity again, because inaccurate words will come in the way. These words have not disappeared as sound waves. They have become sound karma. As sticky sound waves they are hovering around in your mind. This is the main reason why Kabir says that you should not speak about the truth in your heart.

He also consoles you by saying that the knowledgeable have an X-ray vision. They will anyhow know if you are a realised soul. They will peer through the fog of machinations and pretensions and see your heart. If it is true, they will connect enduringly with you.

माली आवत देखि के, कलियां करें पुकार ।
फूली फूली चुनि लई, काल हमारी बार ।।

Kabir says that just as the gardener picks the fully blossomed flowers, the God of death also makes each one of us in this world his morsel. In other words, our blossoming youth is short-lived and death is inevitable.

From time to time, just as all enlightened people do, Kabir also talks of death.

Why do enlightened people talk of death?

Enlightened people talk of death because when you come to terms with the fact that you will die you start living more fully, you are more alive. Secondly, Kabir talks of death also because he knows that the knowledge of our mortality subdues our ego. If, for instance, the average lifespan of man was 500-700 years he would even challenge God. Kabir understands this and so, he often speaks about death.

Kabir knows that death follows him like a shadow, like an angel. He can always feel death by his side. Anytime it can kiss him. And it is the full consciousness of the fact that he will die, which makes him feel one hundred percent alive.

To such enlightened people death is as if sitting next to them and reminding them to do what they do well, not to leave until tomorrow what one can do today, not to entertain feelings of guilt and not to self-loathe. To such people, death becomes a messenger of wisdom. Therefore, in this couplet, when Kabir says that all of us are mortal, he wants to make us consciously realise this fact by bringing us face to face with death, because often, we forget that we have to die.

पात झरन्ता यौं कहै, सुन तरूवर बन राय ।
अबके बिछुड़े ना मिले, दूर पड़ेंगे जाय ।।

Kabir shares what the leaves of the tree say to it as they fall.
They say, that they would drift away so far so as to never meet again.
He is suggesting, the striking similarity to the living beings in this world
who on their demise drift away into an unknown realm,
never to meet again.

Here Kabir is fanning the love in our hearts for our loved ones. There are three kinds of love - *Eros, Filos & Agape.*
Eros means the love between two people.
Filos means the love for learning or knowledge.
Agape means love which does not depend on your liking or disliking - love that flows from you towards everybody, towards the whole universe. It is unconditional love. This type of love has often been described in scriptures.

But Kabir is not talking about this kind of love nor is he talking of Filos. He is talking about Eros - love for another human being. He says that just as two leaves which have fallen and which drift apart; you and your loved one will also drift apart. So make the most of your journey together. Enjoy, revel and soak in love.

कबीर यह गत अटपटी, चटपट लखी न जाय ।
जो मन की खटपट मिटै, अधर भये ठहराय ।।

Kabir attempts to explain the state of higher being and self-realisation.
He admits that it is difficult to express and cannot be seen ordinarily.
However, it is easily achievable without support,
once the mind sheds all doubt and is able to focus itself.

Kabir admits that it is difficult to put in words the higher realisations that you have because this reality, when put in words, changes its nature. Self-realisation is a reality which is soaring in the skies. It is flying. It is touching the clouds. But when you put it in words, these words are metaphorically similar to the hen - a bird which can hop and jump but can't soar. Therefore, Kabir expresses the difficulty to put these realisations into words.

At the same time, he says that these realisations are easily achievable. You don't have to practise rituals; you don't have to follow a guru; they are achievable without support. Your spiritual self is walking side by side with you. You just have to unveil it. And how is it unveiled? When the mind sheds its doubts, develops faith and focuses itself, this spiritual reality is unveiled.

पाहन पूजै हरि मिलै, तो मैं पूजूं पहार ।
ताते तो चक्की भली, पीसि खाये संसार ।।

Kabir rebukes the worship of idols.
He says that if it were possible to come in contact with God
through idols made of stone, I would start worshiping the mountain.
One needs to understand that this is meaningless.
It is better to work your way with a quern than
spend time worshiping these stone-idols,
for the quern grinds the wheat and provides flour that feeds the world
whereas, the idol simply occupies the world space uselessly.

Kabir criticises the worship of idols. For him God is not an anthropomorphic form. He doesn't believe in the image of God (shaped like man) which has been made by man. For him, God is a vibe. God is a force field - a cosmic force field. He says that if you are worshiping idols of stone, he can worship something even bigger. He will start worshiping the mountain. He says a grindstone is better than a stone idol because atleast it grinds wheat and provides flour that feeds the world; the idol just occupies world space uselessly. Idol worship is also detrimental because it binds you to a ritual. Moreover, idol worship can make you fearful.

There is a story of a monk who on a very cold night reached an *ashram* (monastery) and the priest there opened the gates for him and told him that he could go and rest in the temple. The priest then went to his cottage which was warm and slept there. The guest monk was shivering because of the severe cold. Till he saw that the idol in the temple was made of wood. So he burnt that idol. Using the idol as firewood, he warmed himself. The night passed. In the morning, the priest came to the temple and he was aghast at the sight. He was very angry with the guest monk who had burnt down the idol. He threw him out of the ashram for this sacrilege. In the evening, after having reinstalled another idol in the temple and after an elaborate atoning for the blasphemous act done in his temple, the priest decided to go for his walk. As he was walking, he saw near a milestone, this monk who had played havoc at his temple the night before. He was bowing before the milestone, offering flowers and praying. The priest was shocked again. He went up to him and said, "Are you completely crazy? Last night you burned the idol in my temple and now you are praying before this milestone as if it were an idol!" The monk replied, "I am thanking God that he has given me the courage and sight to see and use the idol as firewood when required and to worship and see God's image in this milestone. He has liberated me."

So Kabir knows how idols bind you, how they intimidate you, how they make you fearful and he finds them useless. He finds the grindstone useful. Because Kabir feels action is more important than faith. As Saint James Apostle has said, "What allows us to recognise ourselves as God's children are our deeds, not our faith." He has also said, "Show me your work and I will show you your faith." The quality and the quantity of your work tells how devout a person you are. Rather than lips that pray, Kabir appreciates hands that work for others, hands that heal others.

मन मक्का दिल द्वारिका, काया काशी जान ।
दस द्वारे का देहरा, तामें जोति पिछान ।।

Kabir assures that your mind is the Mecca and
the heart is the door-way to self-realisation.
A sacred and healthy body
may be likened to Kashi the holy place of worship.
This ten door body of the human being is that temple
where self realisation can be attained and
the imperishable soul bears the flames of true knowledge.
In other words, one does not need to go on a pilgrimage to reach God,
the human body is capable of achieving everything right here right now.

By saying that the mind is the Mecca and the heart is the doorway to self-realisation Kabir is simultaneously stressing the importance of the mind and the heart. Mind is the factory of thoughts. Heart is the factory of emotions. When these are in harmony then self-realisation is inevitable.

The third thing that Kabir speaks of is the body. At that time the body was looked down upon, as if it were something soiled, something impure. He says that a healthy body is important. Without a healthy body you can't really be in a state of spiritual bliss. The body is the stadium where the heart and the mind play, where the spiritual game begins. If the stadium is not there the game can't be played. This is the sine-qua-anon of self-realisation. He emphasizes that without the presence of the body there is no spiritual realisation.

Kabir also finds pilgrimages of no use. He says that one does not need to go on pilgrimages. One can achieve everything right here and right now. He finds it meaningless to go on pilgrimages, count beads, keep fasts, and lead the life of an ascetic. All these things are meaningless for him.

In the *Matreyi Upanishad* this thought has been elaborated very well in a shloka (couplet) which says,

Utamah Tatva Chintava, Madhyma Shastra Chintava,
Adhama Mantra Tantra Chintava, Adhmadhamaha Tirth Bhrantatmaha

It means that the superior people are philosophic, the middle level people believe in the scriptures, the people lower than the middle level do *mantras* and *tantras* (chants and rituals) and the lowest people scurry from one pilgrim centre to another looking for God. It depends on your evolution as a spiritual being as to which route and which form of worship will suit you. The highest will be philosophic, the second highest will be scriptural, the third highest will be ritualistic and the fourth highest or the lowest will be wanderers, going from one pilgrim centre to another.

जब तू आया जगत में, लोग हंसे तू रोय ।
ऐसी करनी न करो, पीछे हंसे सब कोय ।।

*Kabir says that when you took birth you cried,
while everyone was happy to see you.
Be careful not to do such deeds that
people express happiness or are thankful when you die.
In other words, live your life such that
You are remembered even when you die.*

Kabir says that when you took birth you cried and everybody rejoiced; it should not so happen that when you die also everybody rejoices. People should remember you well. When you die they should pine for you, only then you have lived a good, meaningful life.

Why would people remember you once you are no more?

To understand this, let us re-visit the three types of love again - *Eros, Filos & Agape*. As explained before, Eros means the love between two people. Filos means the love for learning. And the third type of love, Agape is the love beyond the fact of liking or not liking - the love Jesus spoke of when he said, "Love your enemies," - the love all spiritual Gurus speak of when they say that your love should be unconditional. We will not talk about this third type of love. We will speak about Eros and Filos.

When there is Eros in a relationship, the love between two people, then both are very comfortable with each other. They are comfortable in each other's presence; at the same time, they recognize the other person's potential. It is a comfortable and an enabling presence. When you feel comfortable with somebody and enabled you will miss him.

The other kind of love is Filos (love for learning). Man has had this love for learning since time immemorial. All progress of humanity depends on this love. Those people who leave foot prints through their contributions, who light up many lamps of learning, they are also remembered and even missed.

So, either you should leave warmth and you will be remembered or you should leave traces and tunes which will show the way to others then you will be remembered. It is people who die; relationships like these don't die, they endure.

करैं बुराई सुख चहै, कैसे पावै कोय ।
रोपै पेड़ बबूल का, आम कहां ते होय ।।

Kabir questions that how can someone achieve happiness in life by performing bad deeds?
It is like expecting to get mangoes from a babul tree.
Remember, you reap as you sow.

One really reaps as he sows. I am reminded of a story. A man went to a wishing well. He selected a coin from his wallet and threw it into the well, asking for a beautiful woman. Lo and behold, an extremely pretty woman materialized. Thrilled, he took her to the church, got married to her and subsequently roamed around the town introducing his beautiful wife to one and all. When evening came he was ecstatic at the prospect of making love to his beautiful wife. It was then that she took off her wig and revealed her grey hair, removed her denture and undressed to reveal her wrinkled and sagging body. The man was horrified at the sight and yelled, "I have been cheated by the wishing well. I asked for a beautiful woman and this is what I get?" She replied, "No. You have not been cheated. you threw a false coin in the wishing well. Now come to bed".

So, if one sows a bad seed a bad fruit would come. This is not a make believe matter of stories. It is true in the real world also.

बुरा न देखा बुरा न सुना, बुरा न कैही जोइ ।
जो दिन खोया सब बुरा, मेरा बुरा न होइ ।।

Kabir prophesises that
someone who can eradicate evil from all his senses,
someone who does not see, hear or say anything bad,
will stay protected from the evil attitude of others.

I have come across people who are totally innocent. They are very rare but I have come across such people. And I've found that they are completely immune to being ditched. Nobody has ditched them. Nobody has manipulated or intimidated them. The movie, *Baby's Day Out*, is about a nine-month-old baby from a very rich family who has been kidnapped by three men. This baby, ofcourse, is totally innocent to all the machinations of the kidnappers. And nature helps him in such a way that he stays one step ahead of the kidnappers. The kidnappers keep bumbling and get defeated by the baby again and again. So much so that despite the many dangers that the baby faces he comes out absolutely unscathed.

Kabir speaks about the protective power of this kind of innocence - when there is no evil in any of your senses. That is, if you can't see evil, you can't hear or say anything bad then you will stay protected from the evil attitude of others. Your innocence will become your armour.

Why does this happen?

Firstly, this happens because you are somehow protected by circumstances. And secondly, your innocence makes you blind to what an evil person can do to you. When you are so blinded, then there is no fear and when there is no fear the smell of your apprehension does not reach the evil person. (Usually, it is the smell of fear / weakness which triggers an evil person to attack you).

कबीरा लोहा एक है, गढ़ने में है फेर ।
ताहिका बख़्तर बना, ताहिका समसेर ।।

Kabir says that the same piece of iron
makes the armour for protection and also the sword for slaughter.
The difference is in the intention of the blacksmith.
He implies that it is how man employs his resources
of knowledge, intellect and bodily power that matters.
Man must be able to differentiate between the good and evil
before utilising his resources.

Here Kabir says that the vital element in two things may be the same but how the vital element is moulded will determine what shape it will acquire and what purpose it will be used for or known for. For example, the vital element in both the armour and the sword is iron. One is used for defense the other one is used for attack. And for that matter, the vital element in a cooking pot is also iron but that is used to cook food and to feed others and yourself.

Similarly, the vital element in many people is the same. Let us say, the vital element is any person is his intelligence. His character will determine what he will use his intelligence for. His character is the crucible which will give shape to his intelligence and his intellect. He can use it for the good of others or for the bad; this depends on the teacher, who is metaphorically speaking, the moulder.

तन थिर मन थिर बचन थिर, सुरत निरत थिर होय ।
कहै कबीर इस पलक को, कलप न पायो कोय ।।

Kabir talks of balance of body and heart,
in what you say and how you behave.
It is only through balance that you can achieve
the invaluable wisdom of the world.

Kabir talks about developing a mind of equilibrium. The first step towards such an equanimous mind is to move on the middle path. When you avoid extremes and follow the golden mean then - you are neither a coward nor are you rash, you are courageous; between pride and diffidence you choose modesty; between miserliness and extravagance you choose liberality; between depression and buffoonery you choose good humour and between belligerence and flattery you choose friendship. That essentially means you move towards the mean. In Chinese, there is a word called *Zhong Yong*. Zhong Yong means 'in the middle and in equilibrium'. Hence, the first step to such balance is going towards the way of the mean. The second step is making your utterances close to your behaviour - creating a harmony between your thoughts, words and deeds. In doing so, you start living close to your surface. You become whatever you profess to be. This helps you get rid of any dissonance in your personality. The discord and the cacophony come down. And you reach a state of balance and equilibrium. When you are in this state, you immediately get tuned-in to the universal harmony. The melody of the universe starts playing within you.

मरूं पर मांगू नहीं, अपने तन के काज ।
परमारथ के कारनै, मोहि न आवै लाज ।।

Kabir says it is better to die than to borrow from others.
However, borrowing is not shameful if it is for the welfare of others.

Kabir is against borrowing. In another couplet, he has also said, *"Bin Mange Moti Mile Mange Mile Na Bikh"*. (That is, you get pearls without asking for them, and if you ask, it's like begging and you might not even get alms.) He is against borrowing, however, he says if borrowing is for the welfare of others then it is not shameful and there is no harm in it.

You should be ashamed when you borrow money for your self-interest. But if it is not for yourself then borrowing becomes a welfare measure. Mahatma Gandhi also said the same. Why? Because a man of vision, of noble intentions, may not have money and the man with money, may not have a noble cause to put the money in, he might not even have the time to implement it. This is why Gandhi accepted the gift of land given to him by the white landlord in South Africa where he established his Tolstoy farm.

So when it is for the welfare of others, borrowing may lose the stigma attached to it. Kabir, in this couplet, advises noble people who hesitate to ask, to borrow if it is for a noble cause.

कथनी कथै तो क्या हुआ, करनी ना ठहराय ।
कालबूत का कोट ज्यौं, देखत ही ढहि जाय ।।

Kabir says that true character is
in practicing the wisdom that you preach,
otherwise you are like a paper palace
that falls with the twinkle of an eye.
That is, your downfall is certain.

If you are not practising what you are preaching, your credibility comes down. So anytime you are unable to practise what you preach, and if people raise their eyebrows at that, you must have a very good and true explanation.

Imagine, you are a doctor and an ignorant man comes to you. You realise that he is diabetic, so you tell him to stop taking sweets. Next day, you are in a restaurant enjoying your dessert and he comes in, sees you and says to you, “Doctor, you told me not to have sweets but you are taking sweets to your heart's content”. In this case, you have to explain to him that you are speaking from the other shore. He is a patient and you are healthy that is why you can have desserts and he can't. An explanation is necessary and it must be good. However, in most cases, you should be doing what you say. If you are not, there better be a very good and true explanation otherwise you are going to lose credibility.

The biggest super power in the world, America, is losing credibility today. Why? America says, for example, trade barriers between nations should be demolished. However, its own greatest growth came when it was following very protectionist policies. It is still using subsidies and other protectionist measures to protect its farmers, yet it tells the rest of the world, especially the underdeveloped world, that they should not give subsidies and or impose trade barriers. So the heads of developing countries today are beginning to say, *Don't do as the Americans say, Do as they do.*

It is important to understand that such double-faced people fall from grace, in the twinkle of an eye. When there is lack of congruence between doing and saying, poise is lost. And since poise and great achievement go hand in hand, due to this lack of congruence, these people also lose the prospect of great achievement. Such people call themselves street smart. They are indeed considered smart by some people on the street. But because of lack of character their street never becomes a tarmac and they don't get to soar and master the skies. On the contrary, they often end up as street urchins.

कथनी मीठी खांड सी, करनी विष की लोय ।
कथनी से करनी करै, विष से अमृत होय ।।

Kabir talks of imposters whose
speech is sugar-like, sweet and deeds are poison-like, harmful.
He says, that such people if they observe their speech and actions,
can develop the ability to transform poison to nectar.

Kabir talks about those people whose speech is noble but deeds are ignoble. He says that if such people were to try and transform themselves it would be very easy. This is because on the periphery they are already speaking good things. The only thing is that at heart they are very different from what they claim to be. Kabir says this goodness can travel inwards through words. Words can catalyze the change. Often, first people mend their language, then their behaviour and then this fragrance reaches the insides of their minds and their thoughts start changing.

सांचे कोइ न पतीयई, झूठै जग पतिपाय ।
गली गली गो रस फिरै, मदिरा बैठ बिकाय ।।

Kabir laments that no one has faith in truth
because no one understands its value.
The truthful person is like a milkman
who has to go from house to house to make a sale,
whereas the liar is like a wine seller
who can station himself in one place and his material will sell.

The truth is wholesome but its effect shows over time, whereas a lie is immediately intoxicating. Its short term pleasure will show immediately and its long term ill-effects will take time to manifest. Which is why, the wine seller immediately has an audience and a customer list, whereas the milk seller has to go from house to house to sell his offering.

In Kabir's view (through his life also he showed and demonstrated this), a person selling good things or telling good things should reach out to people. He knows that the priest is self-conscious; Kabir wants him to drop his self consciousness and reach out to people like the milkman does.

Once there was a priest who felt he had a lot to tell the world but because of his shyness could never reach out to an audience. He was extremely knowledgeable and this knowledge and the desire to share it were growing in him. But even when he saw that people were doing wrong he could not reach out to them and say, "Let me teach you the right way," because he felt that this might be seen as arrogant or intrusive or that people might reject him. One day, he was traveling in a bus full of passengers when he got this sudden, very overwhelming urge in him to get up and talk - deliver his message. And he got up and he spoke. People who had to get down (as their bus stops came) kept glued to their seats. They continued their journey to listen to him. After an hour of talking, he finished. The passengers in the bus gave him a standing ovation. He went on to become a great social reformer. Kabir would like the good man to have this courage to sell and tell the world about his products, about his message. Only then, can he really have a much stronger support base for truth, than there is for baser things.

छिमा बड़न को चाहिए, छोटन को उतपात ।
कहाँ विष्णु को घट गयो, जो भृगु मारी लात ।।

Kabir says that a senior person must have the ability to pardon his juniors.
After all, the Supreme God, Vishnu, did not in any way
become less honourable when, as Hindu mythology states,
the Saint Bhrigu, gave him a kick.
Lord Vishnu was quick to forgive him.
To forgive is not a sign of weakness but of great strength.

By fighting with those smaller than you, you define yourself as pettier than what you are. The enemy you engage with, describes you. Your antagonist is your definition also. Because of this reason and out of compassion for those below you and out of understanding that they may be blind or lacking in wisdom, you should forgive these people even when they commit a mistake or offend you. As per Indian mythology, when Saint Bhrighu, reached Vishnu, the Lord of the world, to complain about the severe injustice and torment people were facing because of the demons, he saw that Lord Vishnu was relaxing, as if, unconcerned about his people. Out of anger, Brighu kicked him. But Vishnu overlooked this serious offence and forgave Brighu. This instance Kabir recalls in this couplet. He exhorts you to forgive those who are smaller than you. Ofcourse, this couplet is valid only up to a point.

कबिरा घास न निंदिये, जो पांवों तलि होय ।
उड़ि पडै जब आंख में, खारा दुहेला होय ।।

Kabir cautions against belittling the weak
lest they might cause you irrevocable harm.
Just like kicking the grass under your feet.
If a tiny blade flies into your eyes, it could make you blind.

Kabir is once again invoking your compassion towards the weak by telling you not to underestimate their ability to harm you. Don't kick the grass under your feet, as often the grass can fly into your eyes as you bend down. Kabir also says this, because he knows that the India then, as the India of today, is a very feudalistic society. We tend to misbehave with people who are weaker than us. He knows this tendency of ours and is using this warning to help us curb it.

जाति न पूछो साधु की, पूछि लीजिये ज्ञान ।
मोल करो तरवार का, पड़ी रहन दो म्यान ।।

Kabir says that when inquiring about the credentials of a saint
or a learned man don't ask about his caste or creed
but seek his vast knowledge.
Just like it is advisable to value the sword,
but worrying about the quality of the sheath is unnecessary.

Kabir says focus on the content that the Saint talks of. Don't focus on where the Saint is coming from or what is his style or what are his credentials, caste or creed. Focus on the knowledge he has. Style, credentials, creed, caste - all these are like the sheath. Content is the sword. Do not be taken in by appearances. Focus on content to estimate the intrinsic value of the Saint.

कामी क्रोधी लालची, इनते भक्ति न होय ।
भक्ति करै कोई सूरमा, जाति बरन कुल खोय ।।

Kabir proclaims that people caught up in carnal desires,
people who easily lose their temper or are greedy;
will never be able to generate devotion in themselves.
It is only those who can rise above caste, religion and lineage
and see everyone with the same respect,
who can bring themselves to that blissful state of prayer.

According to Kabir, three types of people cannot devote themselves to worship - Those who are caught up in carnal desires, those who are greedy and those who lose their temper easily. Those who are caught in carnal desires or who are caught in greed get entangled in a never-ending web. For instance, when you engage in sex often, your appetite for sex increases. The more you have of it, the more you want it. Same is true for money. You are caught in a trap which is like an unstoppable merry-go-round. You can't get off it. Now you don't get the time or the opportunity to follow the path of devotion.

People who lose their temper easily, they too find it difficult to follow the path of devotion, because when you lose your temper you are off-key. When you lose your temper you bend on one extreme, you rave and rant and shout and hit and then another extreme takes over - of guilt and resentment. So you keep oscillating like a pendulum from one end to the other. You don't come to a state of poise. And that state of poise is necessary for this path of devotion.

Kabir also emphasizes that those who wish to follow the path of devotion or reach the blissful state of prayer, should rise above the status trappings of caste, lineage and religion. Especially religion, since it takes you towards ritualism and serves a as barrier to devotion. The orthodoxy of religion binds you; you become unavailable to the spiritual experience.

सातों सायर मैं फिरा, जंबू द्वीप दौ पीठ ।
निंद पराइ ना करै, सो कोइ बिरला दीठ ।।

Kabir informs that he has crossed the seven seas and traveled world over.
He laments that everywhere he went;
he found that people were quick to defame or pull the others down.

Wherever you go in the world, there is this tendency to defame or pull others down. Kabir talks about this tendency. It comes from competition. From our childhood we are taught to compete. As infants if we were not walking as soon as the neighbour's child started walking, we were pushed by our parents to WALK. If we were not talking and the neighbour's child was, we were forced by our parents to TALK. So this competition is deeply engrained in human psyche through conditioning.

Often, you criticize or pull down somebody because you feel that if you do not criticize or pull him down in front of someone, then he might do so when you are not around. So when he is spoken of, you cut him down. Maybe gently, but you do cut him down so as to neutralize any criticisms which may come from him about you. And this, "Doing unto others before they do anything to you" is a tactic which is prevalent all over the world, though a little more in the East than in the West. Why? Maybe because the population is more in the East, so competition is greater. And so the feeling of jealousy is also accentuated. This desire to defame or pull down somebody comes because of jealousy and competition. And possibly because resources are scarce and competition is intense, this tactic is more prevalent in the East. Another point, in the East, status is very important. When status becomes very important then, at all times, you keep nudging to improve your position. You are jostling all the time. It is said, that big people become big by making others big but small people become big by making others small. It is this latter weakness which is what Kabir is talking about, the desire to pull down the other person so that you can seem bigger or taller in comparison to him.

सायर नाहीं सीप बिन, स्वाति बूंद भी नाहिं ।
कबीर मोती नीपजै, सुन्नि सिसिर गढ़ माहिं ।।

Kabir says that despite the fact that there are no sea shells on a mountain top, nor does it rain pearls there, precious gems are often gathered from the peaks of mountains.

Kabir's gems are symbolic of the spiritually enlightened saints and sages who choose to meditate on mountain tops. Confucius has also said that clever people like the seas and virtuous people like the mountains. Perhaps, it is the ethereal silence of the mountains, which is its biggest invitation card, its greatest attraction. The sea is noisy. If you have been on the shores of a sea at night, when other sounds are absent, you will hear the din of the sea. In comparison, there is a solacing silence in the mountains. The vibe of the mountains resonates with the spiritual and that is why the spiritual are often attracted to the mountains.

जग में बैरी कोय नहीं, जो मन शीतल होय ।
या आपा को डारि दे, दया करे सब कोय ।।

Kabir enlightens you with the thought that
if your mind is calm,cool and composed
then it will not engage in altercations with anyone and
you will not have any enemies in this world.
It is imperative to negate your ego and
you will receive love and kindness from everyone.

Here Kabir shares how to transcend enmity, transcend belligerence within us. He says that if your mind is calm, cool and composed then you will have no altercations with anyone. He points to the fact that the reason for a fight, disagreement or for discord is not the other person. The reason is within you.

In Jainism, there is a mantra called the *Namokar mantra*. It's a salutation to five types of masters. Here I'll share the salutation to the first type (*Arihantas*- the highest kind of masters) as that is relevant to this couplet. Arihantas are those who have no enemies, those who have conquered all opposing beings, as well as, discordant thoughts and have come to a state of total poise.

How does one become an Arihanta?

By changing the vibrations of your mind and taking them to another level, taking them from competition and possessiveness to an all embracing kind of frequency. The change which the Arihanta sees in the world is not because the world has changed but because his mind has changed. As someone has said correctly, we don't see the world as the world is - we see the world as we are. Once Abraham Lincoln was told by a lady, “Why are you referring to these opponents of yours as friends? They are our enemies and should be destroyed.” Abraham Lincoln said, “By calling them my friends and by making them my friends, am I not destroying my enemies?” The important thing to note here is that before you call them your friends you need to see them as friends - which is what Lincoln was capable of doing.

So sometimes you have to engage with your enemies and win. Sometimes you have to disengage and win them over. Kabir here is talking about that disengaged, equanimous state of mind.

कुंभै बांधा जल रहै, जल बिन कुंभै न होय ।
ज्ञानै बांधा मन रहै, मन बिनु ज्ञान न होय ।।

Kabir says that water stays in a pitcher because the pitcher is designed so,
and without mixing clay with water, a pitcher cannot be made -
Implying, that it is because of being in collaboration with each other
that they both exist.
Similarly, a restless mind can be quietened if
tied with the strings of true knowledge and
at the same time, true knowledge and wisdom is possible only
with the help of the mind.

Here Kabir says that true knowledge and mind exist in collaboration. Without the mind you cannot get true knowledge. Kabir challenges the Eastern belief that one should drop the mind. It takes a lot of courage to challenge this belief because the seers in India have been, from time immemorial, stressing, drop the mind. Maybe there has been an ulterior motive here. The Guru wants you to drop the mind because he feels that if you keep your mind on, you might see through his shallowness and his sham. Or he is just parroting 'drop-the-mind-drop-the-mind' because that is what he has heard. The East has decried the mind. India, thanks to our Gurus, has especially looked down upon the mind and this insult to the mind has hurt us very badly. Inspite of having such a cerebral population, India, in the last 1000 years hasn't come out with any tangible innovation, presented to the world as our own. We do claim that we discovered this and that, but where is our contribution. The steam engine was invented in the West, the car was invented in the West, electricity was invented in the West, telephony was invented in the West, air-conditioning was invented in the West, the airplane was invented in the West, space travel happened for the first time in the West. We have a glorious past but where is our recent contribution?

That is why I say, don't drop the mind sharpen the mind. If you sharpen the mind, you can also reach the same no-mind state which is the goal of spirituality. How? As you sharpen the mind, it is so sharp, eventually, that one of its facets is super sharp and the other facet is a no-mind. You can switch to that no-mind state just like that. And because you have sharpened the mind, on the way, you will release byproducts. You will cut an album, write a book, make a movie, you will release traces and tunes, come out with inventions because these are byproducts of the mind. So by reaching that no-mind realm through the sharpening of the mind route you will do well in this world and also in what is called the other world.

आव गया आदर गया, नैनके गया सनेह ।
यह तीनो तबही गये, जबही कहा कछू देह ।।

*Kabir warns that man should desist from the habit of asking favours,
as it dries up the lubricant of love and respect
that has been built in a relationship.*

According to Kabir, love in a relationship arises from selflessness and respect from dignity. If you ask for favours again and again you are no longer selfless, the relationship has become purely utilitarian for you. Also, you are losing dignity and therefore respect. Thus, he warns you to desist from the habit of asking for favours. Though, he warns you to desist from the habit, he doesn't say that you should never ask for favours. Just that if you get in the habit you will erode love and respect.

Kabir was a very self-respecting person. He has also said in his other writings that you should not go to places where you are not welcome because this will lead to erosion of your self-esteem. In one of his couplets, he says that if the lady of the house keeps enquiring about the reason of your visit and the man refers to your father by his last name you will be hurt and your self-esteem will be eroded. He has also said in one of his popular couplets that familiarity breeds contempt. Do not become too familiar with your friends otherwise again you will lose respect.

कबीर तहां न जाइये, जहां जो कुल को हेत ।
साधुपनो जानै नहीं, नाम बाप को लेत ।।

Kabir says that refrain from visiting family and relatives who do not value your achievements, wisdom and status.

Like Jesus, Kabir understands that a Prophet is never respected in his home town. When Jesus went to his hometown with his disciples the people there insulted him. Why? They insulted him because they were not willing to give the new found status of a spiritual guru to Jesus. They ridiculed him as the son of a carpenter and called him names. When his disciples asked him, "Why do they treat you like this master?" Jesus said, "A prophet is never respected in his hometown." It is because the feeling of jealousy is the strongest in your hometown. Among two businessmen who have grown up together or who know each other, the smaller one would be jealous of the other businessman friend who is doing better than him. But do you think the first businessman would be jealous of the Tatas, Ambanis or Bill Gates. No. They are not in his scheme of things. They are outside his jealousy circle. Jesus was in the jealousy circle of the residents of that town. You are in the jealousy circle of your closest relatives and friends. That is why they are most jealous of you.

Not only jealousy, there is another feeling also that operates here. The relatives or friends may feel insecure, that a person from among their group has risen so high that it is no longer possible to interact with him closely. So they try to dilute his status. Kabir says that such people are the last to accept you as a man of learning and that you should refrain from visiting such people who do not value your achievements, wisdom and status.

हस्ती चढ़िए ज्ञान की, सहज दुलीचा डार ।
स्वान रूप संसार है, भूंकन दे झकमार ।।

Kabir advises you to continue trekking up and
spreading the carpet of true knowledge freely
without worrying about what others say.
The world is like an ignorant dog which has the habit of barking.
Eventually, it will tire and become silent.

Here Kabir is asking you to follow your dream, to follow your calling, without worrying what others will say. Others always have to say something.

There is a story about an old man, his son and their donkey. They were going from their village to another. The father was sitting astride on the donkey and the son was walking alongside. Some people crossed them and they spoke among themselves, within earshot of this trio, saying, "What kind of a father is this - he is enjoying the ride while his son has to trudge?" Hearing this, the father got down and made the son ride the donkey. A little distance ahead another group of people crossed them and this group commented, "What a shameless and selfish son - he is making the old man walk while he is riding on the donkey." When the father and the son heard this, they decided to ride the donkey together and now both of them sat on the donkey's back. Another group of people passed them by. One of them commented, "What cruel owners of this donkey these are - both sitting together on one poor animal." Hearing this, the father and son got down from the donkey and started walking alongside the donkey. Another group of people crossed and these people said, "They are really stupid people - the donkey is there and still they are walking - they could have ridden the donkey." Not knowing what to do, the father and son took a long bamboo pole and tied the donkeys legs to the pole. They put either ends of the pole on their respective shoulders and started walking. The donkey was hanging upside down on the pole which was resting on the father's and the son's shoulder. Yet another group of people crossed them and they found the site shocking. They said, "The father and the son are truly crazy." And this time they were on a bridge. A river was flowing below. The donkey was also in quite a precarious situation not knowing what to do he was flaying his hind and fore limbs. And because of this tussle all of them fell into the river and died.

What is the moral of the story?

The moral of the story is no matter what you do, people will say something or the other. And if you start going by what they say then they know that they have a remote control on you. Then they know that they can wind you and unwind you with their comments. So Kabir says, do what you think you must do. Be guided by your conscience and logic. Don't worry about the world's adverse comments. Eventually, once they know that your resolve is strong and you are not affected by their comments, they will get tired and stop commenting.

कैसा भी सामर्थ्य हो, बिन उद्यम दुख पाय ।
निकट असन बिन कर चले, कैसे मुख में जाय ।।

Kabir says that no matter how powerful a person is,
he has to suffer unless he is industrious.
The food may be kept before you, but it will not go into your mouth
unless you make use of your hands.
That is, one has to make efforts in order to be able to accomplish a deed.

Here Kabir expresses another very radical truth for India. He says, no matter how talented you are if you do not work hard you will not be successful.

Why is it a radical truth?
Because there are two traditions in India - One is the *Brahmana* Tradition and the other is the *Shramana* Tradition. The Brahmana tradition says that what is to be is to be. Your destiny decides everything. Your effort is not of consequence. And the Shramana Tradition says that your effort is most important. The result will depend on your effort. Unfortunately, it has been India's great misfortune that we have believed too much in the Brahmana tradition and very little in the Shramana tradition. Infact, the Shramana tradition for decades and centuries, got overpowered and gagged by the Brahmana tradition. Belief in the supernatural and superstition grew because of this tradition. When the Mughal invaders first came to India, folklore says, thousands of Hindu men rather than resisting the invasion, went to Mount Kailash to pray and perform rituals before Lord Shiva (mythologically Mount Kailash is considered Shiva's abode) so that

he would open his third eye and turn the Mughals to ashes. After several months of rituals, when nothing happened, they returned to their homes only to realise that not only had the Mughals established themselves as the new rulers but had also taken away their wives.

Kabir is a man of wisdom. He speaks on behalf of the Shramana tradition in this couplet. Unless you move, results will not come. And he understands why it is so much more comfortable to believe in the Brahamana tradition. It's because the Brahamana tradition does not force you to work. It appeals to our instinct for laziness. And it tries to come out with fantastic promises and procedures. It says that it will take you from Point A to Point B even without expending any effort. It is against this tradition that he is speaking. The truth of almost every successful man that I have met is that without effort, success eludes you.

In fact, the right attitude is to wait for the universe to sing your song. But meanwhile, all the time, practise painstakingly on your keyboard. So that when the universe breaks into a song for you, you are ready to add your music to its lyrics. Hard work is desire with its hands to the plough. It is a powerful magnet to universal energy. Hard work attracts whatever universal energy there is. When the clouds see you sweat they are also tempted to rain. Kabir underlines the importance of hard work. It's not that Kabir does not believe in luck. But he knows that even to take advantage of good luck one has to work hard. If your sail boat is parked at the shore, how will you benefit from favourable winds? If you have not practised sailing, how would you adjust the sails when the winds blow in your favour? Chances are, that if your senses have rusted due to disuse you might not even be able to recognize the favourable wind. To be able to spot your lucky chance as well as to exploit it, you have to strive, you have to work hard.

श्रम ही ते सब होत है, जो मन राखै धीर ।
श्रम ते खोदत कूप ज्यों, थल में प्रगटै नीर ।।

Kabir believes that it is only through hard work and patience that one achieves success.
It is hard work that helps get water from the bottom of the earth.
Perseverance and endurance are the key to success.

Here again Kabir speaks about hard work and perseverance. He says if you are digging a well, then you will indeed reach the water spring - you have to just go on digging. I would go so far as to say, that if you are digging the well and still you don't hit water, still go on digging - you might hit oil, by selling which you can own not just a few water wells; you can own some lakes.

So do not give up. If you know that the direction which you have taken is right, go on persevering.

धीरे धीरे रे मना, धीरे सब कुछ होये ।
माली सींचे सौ घड़ा, रितु आये फल होये ।।

Kabir says that the universe moves at its own pace.
You cannot force the speed of the universe, just as
you cannot make a seed sprout by pouring hundred buckets of water on it.
It will sprout only when spring comes.

This verse comes from a deep understanding of how the universe functions. Kabir knows that the universe moves at its own pace. You can't force the speed of the universe. So he advises you to be patient. He believes in perseverance, not persistence. Persistence can sometimes be counterproductive and sometimes worthless. Imagine you are a doctor and an infertile couple comes to you and without going into the details of the case you tell them to persist, to just go on doing it. Do you think they would be successful through persistence? Nothing will happen. You have to find out what is the problem, why is it that the woman can't conceive and so on. There is some kind of an insistence in persistence. Though persevering is a mark of determination, insistence is more like stubbornness that tries to dismantle the rhythm of the universe. Insistence can be counterproductive. You should return to your battles, to your struggles, to your pursuits not out of stubbornness but when you sense that the weather is favourable. Otherwise display patience; work patiently, and persevere patiently - not stubbornly.

नवन नवन बहु अंतरा, नवन नवन बहु बान ।
ऐ तीनों बहुतै नबै, चीता चोर कमान ।।

Kabir points out that bowing down is not the same thing as humility. He cites the case of the hunter, the leopard and the thief who bow down too much but with evil intentions. He implies that one should beware of such people.

Kabir speaks about false humilities - gestures which can be mistaken for humility but actually have evil intentions; intentions to deceive. Sometimes people will be humble with you only to get your favour, at other times, people might be humble because there is no other option for them. This is not true humility. For example, many people in old age acquire what I call, geriatric humility. This humility comes to them as they age. It does not spring from any transformation within. It stems from the deterioration of physical strength. To be able to carry your ego you need a certain kind of aggression which requires physical robustness and for most people with age this sturdiness withers. So they have no option but to be humble. This humility is not born of any evolution or transformation. It comes because of osteoporosis. It is a fake humility.

There is another type of humility, which springs from the ego itself, where a powerful person poses to be humble. This powerful, yet humble image gets him even more attention because of the contrast in the image people say, "So powerful yet so humble!" This kind of humility prepares a feast for the ego. It is a subtle game that ego plays here. This type of humility is also artificial. In fact it is hypocritical. It is a sham which often, you might not be aware that you are carrying. Golda Meir was referring to this type of humility when she told a man who was so posing, "Don't be so humble, after all you are not that great."

Then, there is the humility of copying. Some person says, it is very important to be humble. You look here and there. There is no other opinion coming through. You also start saying yes-yes, it is very important to be humble and the whole neighbourhood starts saying that it is very important to be humble and everybody starts behaving humbly. But it is only a sham.

All these are artificial humilities and Kabir warns you against these.

प्रीति ताहि सो कीजिये, जो आप समाना होय ।
कबहुक जो अवगुन पड़ै, गुन ही लहै समोय ।।

Kabir advises that you should only love / befriend someone who shares with you a similar value system. He should be someone who can forgive your follies and remember your virtues at a time when you unknowingly make a mistake.

Here Kabir speaks about the importance of looking for a similar value system, a similar world view when choosing a friend. A friend should also be able to overlook the occasional erratic behaviour coming from you because he knows it is not your nature. He should not have the desire to retaliate in kind but should greet your tantrum with silence, taking a macro view of the relationship. When he does this, your tantrum is just a small blip on a large screen. Overall, the relationship between you and him is fulfilling for both the parties. It is a rich canvas of mutually nourishing feelings just stained in a little corner. When he looks at your tantrum this way, this view will generate understanding and will give him reasons why he should not allow the stain to spread. At such trying times, he should remember your virtues, your goodness and your consistency.

राम बुलावा आया तो, कबीरा दे दिया रोए ।
जो सुख साधु संगत में, बैकुंठ में न होए ।।

Kabir says that the company of good men is so fulfilling and satisfying that one would not want to lose them even for heaven.

Kabir shares how fulfilling it is to be in the company of good people. And he says, "God has called me to heaven but I am not interested in going. I am really enjoying with my good friends (good people)." For him this communion with good people (Satsang) is more important and better than salvation. He has found good people and he has experienced the bliss of their company. This couplet is coming from that blissful experience.

या दुनिया में आइके, छाड़ि देय तू ऐंठ ।
लेना है सो लेइ लै, उठी जात है पैंठ ।।

Kabir stresses on the need to disregard or give up ego and arrogance.
Life is too short and one should take initiative
and work towards achievement and not haughtiness.

Kabir tells you to focus on achievement. Don't let your position or status overpower your functioning. Your work is more important. Whenever there is a tendency of your success going to your head, try to look at things in their perspective. Try to look at people who have been much more successful than you. This will bring down your ego.

Try also to see your position in the overall scheme of things. Once Socrates was sitting in his school with several of his students and an extremely rich and famous man of Athens entered the hall to meet him. Socrates was engrossed in his discussion, so didn't notice his arrival. The man felt affronted but still decided to wait a while. However, with every passing minute his anger was rising. After about half an hour of waiting, teething with anger, he suddenly shouted at Socrates, "You don't know who I am". Socrates looked at his visitor and said, "Let us decide that also." He called for a world map and asked this man to point out where Athens was in the map. After a careful scrutiny the man pointed to a little speck on the map. Socrates then asked him to point out on the map where his estate was, where his palace was and so on. The man now realised that those possessions that he was so proud of were specks within specks in the larger scheme of things, and he came to terms with his own insignificance. The lesson was completed. Socrates folded the map and handed it over to the man as a reminder of his humble status in the world.

Focus on your achievement and the rest will take care of itself. You will get your position in the society. You don't have to arrogantly claim it. It will come. Your legitimate due will be given to you. Even if not in your lifetime; if you focus on achievement you would leave your footprints on the sands of time and no breeze will be able to erase them.

बड़ा बड़ाई ना करै, छोटा बहु इतराय ।
ज्यौं प्यादा फरजी भया, टेढ़ा टेढ़ा जाय ।।

Kabir says the wise do not self praise,
only the foolish in trying to appear wise, keep blowing their own trumpet
and in the process expose their foolishness.
It is like a pawn trying to move like the bishop.
It is against the rules of the game.

Kabir says do not be seduced by your self importance. It is not the whistle that pulls the train. Also when you start crowing, you stop growing. When you blow your own trumpet, not only does it look awkward, and not only do you make a spectacle of yourself, you also bring down or erect barriers to the feedback which could have come on your way or which could have helped you improve on your follies. People would think that you are so smitten by yourself that you will not be able to take any constructive criticism also.

Moreover, soldiers of a General who brags, have few attainments. Therefore, by blowing your own trumpet, you weaken your team also. They start focusing on praising you rather than on producing results. Kabir says even Lord Indra is looked down upon when he praises himself. So avoid blowing your own trumpet, focus on achievements and contributions.

शब्द गुरू का शब्द है, काया का गुरू काय ।
भक्ति करै नित शब्द की, सत्गुरू यौं समुझाय ।।

Kabir says that only words can highlight the importance of words,
just like it is only the body through which
one may acquire knowledge of the body.
He advises all to worship the words of true wisdom
for an absolute experience of mind and body.

Kabir speaks about the importance of words. Today it is fashionable to say, “I've had such a divine experience that it cannot be put in words” or “I would not like to spoil it by putting it in words.” Indeed, there are some experiences which cannot be put in words. Still we must try. Because when we try to describe things which the existing vocabulary cannot describe, we end up expanding the vocabulary. And Kabir understands this.

Did you know that in the Bible there are only three colours - the whole Bible mentions only three colours. Do you think that the number of colours was less at that time? Was it only three? No. There were as many colours then as there are today, but man did not have the vocabulary to name those colours. Imagine if people had said that the other colours are indescribable, they can't be put into words; then we would not have had the nomenclature for the other colours. So we should try to stretch the boundary of language so that it describes what is considered indescribable today. That's why Kabir highlights the importance of words. Only through words, will you come to know the reality. Actually words are the currency of thought. You can't think without words. And Kabir in this couplet is giving words their due.

माया मुई न मन मुआ, मरि मरि गया शरीर ।
आशा तृष्णा ना मुई, यौं कथि कहैं कबीर ।।

Kabir states that in this cycle of life and death, greed, attachments, expectations and ambitions do not come to an end. In such a scenario, how can one attain fulfillment or self realisation?

In this couplet, Kabir utters another radical truth - desires do not come to an end. You might go, but desires live on. This is what avant-garde psychology is saying today - That desire is the fabric of life. It says, "If you desire something passionately then, you will definitely get it." It is not asking you to give up desire, on the contrary, it is asking you to intensify desire. Western psychology has understood that desire cannot be done away with. Infact instead of suppressing desire, it should be utilized. Moreover, if reincarnation is a truth, it has to do something with desire.

And in a country like India, where desire has always been looked down upon, Kabir had the guts to say that it is permanent, it won't go.

टालै टूलै दिन गयो, ब्याज बढ़न्ता जाय ।
ना हरि भजा ना खत कटा, काल पहुंचा आय ।।

Kabir says that we pass our lives putting off things for the future. In the process, we keep accumulating the baggage of our sins, not fulfilling our responsibilities and ignoring our spiritual life, only to regret when the time of death comes.

Here Kabir is cautioning you not to keep putting things off for the future. There are two things which are very important in Kabir's worldview. One is spiritual growth and the other is fulfilling your responsibilities. He says you should fulfill your responsibilities, make your contributions to your family, to your society, as well as strive for spiritual growth. Only then you have lived a good life. Otherwise, when the time of death comes you will have a deep sense of regret that you let it all slip away. The opportunity called life was given to you and you kept sitting on the shore. You could have dived into the ocean to get the pearls and a rich experience but you were cowardly and ungrateful to the gift of life. You kept sitting on the shore and life slipped like sand through your fingers.

बालपन भोले गया, और जुवा महमंत ।
वृद्धपने आलस गयो, चला जरन्ते अंत ।।

Kabir points to a life where the childhood is spent in innocence,
the youth in hedonistic involvements and
old age in idle nothingness and sorrow.
Such a life when being taken for its last rituals,
wonders how and what became of it.

Kabir warns you. He says that childhood goes away in innocence and you can't do anything about it because your innocence is a barrier to rational thought (at that age). But once you are an adult, you must watch yourself. Don't lose your youth in hedonistic pleasures of the flesh. If you go in for too much hedonism then your old age will be difficult because the repercussions of hedonism might strike, disease might strike. If youth is spent carefully then, even in old age you can contribute. And then that deep regret of having wasted life, as mentioned before, does not exist. As death approaches, you go satisfied. You played your innings. You did your job. If there is a God, when you meet him, He will say, "Well done."

Other Books by PAVAN CHOUDARY

World acclaimed book,
When You Are Sinking Become A Submarine

Rs. 245/- 184p Pub: Wisdom Tree

Available in Hindi as

Rs. 150/- 186p Pub: WVPD

It's the first time I've ever read anything like it, and I imagine it's the best introduction. I really enjoy how he looks at people, and I'm learning a lot... I tell people, don't go with Eckhart Tolle just because Oprah says you should. Go with someone who does it because they honestly have something interesting to say."

- Carolyn Marcille (Barnes & Noble, New York, USA)

Pavan Choudary is also the author of **The RX Factor**-A Path Breaking Business Book.
For more details, testimonials, Indian & International press coverage, visit **www.starcoach.co.in**

Other Books by Wisdom Village Publications Division (WVPD)

This handbook to drugless therapies envisions to empower you with the energy to heal yourself and others around you through the remarkable healing powers of Acupressure and Magneto Therapy.

Dr. Anand P.Verma
Healing In Your Hands
Rs. 250/- 222p ISBN978-81-906555-1-4

To book your orders:
E-mail: wisdomvillageindia@gmail.com
or call +91 9811514287

FORTHCOMING Books by **Wisdom Village (Publications Division)**

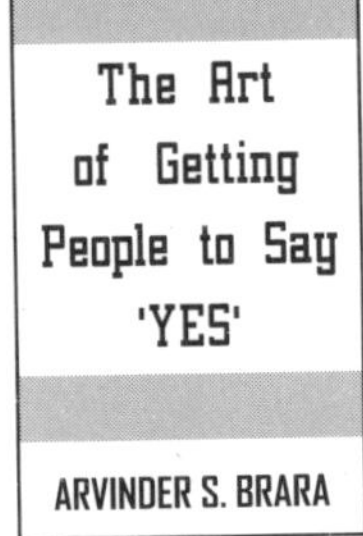

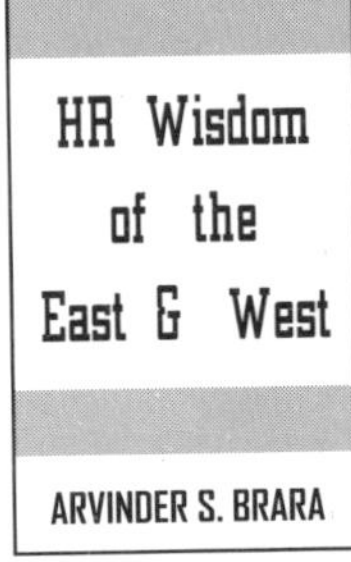

Vivekacharya School of Wisdom & Success (VSWS), the educational off-shoot of Wisdom Village is achieving new milestones in the fields of Wisdom and attitudinal training across the country and beyond. VSWS has successfully conducted workshops on **The Art of Wise Leadership, Success Management, Secrets of Success, Winning Through Wisdom & Creativity** and many more for the **University of Sydney, TiE, India Club (Australia), Singapore Management University, Bill & Melinda Gates Foundation, Tata Power, IFFCO, Max New York Life, Apollo International, European Business Group, Rotary International**... the list is endless.

Announcing Programs for Corporates / Academic / Management Institutes in 2009:

1. **WISDOM & SUCCESS IN INTERVIEWS**
   A special half day program @ the cost of a movie ticket, Rs. 200 per student (minimum requirement 200 students)
2. **GROWTH & DEVELOPMENT PROGRAM**
   A unique 5 day program, spread over 5 weekends @ the cost of Rs. 1000 per student (minimum requirement 200 students)
3. **A TRANSFORMATIONAL GROWTH & DEVELOPMENT PROGRAM**
   Especially designed for Middle & Senior Managers. To hone their political, social, material and spiritual intelligence.

For Bookings & more details please contact:

Email: wisdomvillageindia@gmail.com   Phone: +91 98115.14287

SUCCESS SUTRAS FOR THE 21ST CENTURY : A TRILOGY OF WISDOM

- ☐ **Chanakya's Political Wisdom**
- ☑ **Confucius' Social Wisdom**
- ☐ **Kabir's Spiritual Wisdom**

Presenting

Confucius' Social Wisdom

SUCCESS SUTRAS FOR THE 21ST CENTURY : A TRILOGY OF WISDOM

- ☐ Chanakya's Political Wisdom
- ☑ Confucius' Social Wisdom
- ☐ Kabir's Spiritual Wisdom

VIVEKACHARYA PAVAN CHOUDARY

Wisdom Guru

&

Author of the world acclaimed book -

When You Are Sinking Become a Submarine

A WVPD ORIGINAL

Books from Wisdom Village (Publications Division) envision to enhance and enrich its readers with life changing experiences from the mind, body and soul genres. They strive towards holistic development.

Editorial Coordinator — Charushilla Narula
Design — Arpan Advertising & Marketing

First published 2009

 This book is part of the three books in the Trilogy of Wisdom by Vivekacharya Pavan Choudary.

ISBN 978-81-906555-4-5

Published by:

Wisdom Village (Publications Division)
Knowledge is information. Wisdom is transformation.

WVPD is a part of Wisdom Village
124 Satya Niketan
IInd Floor,
New Delhi - 110021
Email: wisdomvillageindia@gmail.com
Contact Person: Charushilla Narula

CONTENTS

ABOUT VIVEKACHARYA PAVAN CHOUDARY

Vivekacharya Pavan Choudary is a world icon in Success Coaching, Political thinking & Practical Spirituality. He has been acknowledged for his global contributions in the fields of Wisdom, Leadership, Management, Psychology, Creativity, State Craft & Spirituality. Today he is among the foremost thinkers of the world in breadth and depth of thinking. By sharing his ideas and insights he has contributed to the success of sportstars, film stars, CEOs and the political elite both in India and abroad. So pioneering are his thoughts that they have initiated a wave of social reform, which is gradually adding to the national fabric.

His world acclaimed book, 'When You Are Sinking Become a Submarine', expounds a new philosophy of power and success. It has crossed Indian shores and is becoming a reference text for leaders worldwide. It has already been translated in Hindi (Aisa Paal Taane ki Aandhi Urja Bane) and editions in other languages are soon to be launched.

A leader, on the path of nation building Vivekacharya has moved from strength to strength and today he is being viewed as the most promising political thinker and management speaker, shaping opinions on practically all aspects of governance, social reform and leadership. Not a pundit but a successful practitioner, Vivekacharya Pavan Choudary, is the CEO and MD of Vygon, a leading French Multinational in the field of Healthcare.

Considering his unmatched profile and the quality of his research in the fields of socio-politico-spiritual wisdom, it was only apt for WVPD to request him to compile this unique **Trilogy of Wisdom**, a path-breaking commentary on Chanakya's Political Wisdom, Confucius' Social Wisdom and Kabir's Spiritual Wisdom.

For more details on the author and to order other titles please visit www.starcoach.co.in

A NOTE FROM THE PUBLISHER

Wisdom Village (Publications Division) (WVPD) proudly presents SUCCESS SUTRAS FOR THE 21ST CENTURY: A TRILOGY OF WISDOM By VIVEKACHARYA PAVAN CHOUDARY. This is a unique rendition (in print and audio) of **Chanakya's Political Wisdom, Confucius' Social Wisdom and Kabir's Spiritual Wisdom** as has never been presented before. It is an attempt to make the wisdom of these great masters relevant to us today.

Vivekacharya Pavan Choudary, in this epic-like trilogy, accompanied with its soul-stirring audio version, provides a ready guide to achieving Political sharpness, Social order and Spiritual bliss.

CONFUCIUS & VIVEKACHARYA

One of the most intriguing sources of Confucius' writing is his analects. Vivekacharya Pavan Choudary, who has been nominated as the Vice President for the Asian Creativity Association, based out of Shanghai, China and who has himself studied sociological intelligence and development in great depth, gives a contemporary social dimension to these Analects.

Moreover, his in-depth understanding of social units, societies and their dynamics has allowed Vivekacharya to interpret and provide a modern-day perspective to the wisdom of Confucius.

Confucius was a strong advocate of action versus idle thought, and believing in the same ideals, in the following commentary, Vivekacharya Pavan Choudary provides the basis for enduring societal prosperity and harmony.

Charushilla Narula
wisdomvillageindia@gmail.com

INTRODUCTION

In China it is said that for the well-being of the body, follow Taoism; for the wellbeing of the soul follow Buddhism and for the well-being of the society follow Confucianism.

Confucius was a sage and social philosopher of China whose teachings have deeply influenced East Asia, including China, Korea, and Japan for two thousand five hundred years. The relationship between Confucianism and Confucius himself, however, is tenuous. Confucius' ideas were not accepted during his lifetime as the Chinese society was a decadent society that was seeped in Taoism, that talked of idleness. Confucius came and he talked of duty, he talked of action and not just idle action, but wise action...that leads to a happy populace and restores social order.

Confucius' Social Wisdom is a phenomenal amalgamation of Confucian understanding and Vivekacharyan interpretation of human nature:

How should a person behave as the unit of a family, a society member and as a ruler?
How social relationships can be brought in harmony?
Why some societies succeeded while the others failed?
What can India learn from successful and prosperous societies?

The reading is aimed at opening your window to harmonious relationships.

Enjoy.

Social Wisdom of Confucius

Natural instinct enables a man
to understand the way of Heaven through sincerity.
Education enables him to be sincere
through understanding the way of Heaven.
Sincerity ensures understanding
and understanding guarantees sincerity.

Confucius is for the society and for the nation which is why the first thing that he asks for is sincerity. Sincerity in the Confucian meaning has three fragments - loyalty (the foremost fragment), integrity and honesty.

By loyalty, Confucius means faithfulness. By integrity, he means doing the right thing. And by honesty he means telling the truth. However, Confucius understands that one can be honest without being high on integrity. For instance, imagine you have gone on an official tour. You come back and submit an expense statement which is inflated. You are reimbursed the money, however, your conscience starts pricking you and one day you go to your boss and confess the truth. You own up. In such a case, even though you have been honest you have not been high on integrity. For Confucius, doing the right thing and telling the truth both are important. So for him sincerity means faithfulness, doing the right thing and telling the truth.

He says sincerity is the way of heaven. By way of heaven, he means the Tao - the guiding force of the universe, the guiding principle of the universe. In other words, it implies that once you are sincere you come in sync with the guiding principle of the universe.

Then he says to strive to be sincere is the way of man. He means, it is human to strive to be sincere. It is in the nature of man to move towards sincerity. Interestingly, even in this century one of the leading proponents of Psychology, Martin Seligman, who has studied Happiness in great detail, has come to a similar conclusion. He says that happiness has little to do with pleasure and much to do with developing personal strengths and character. Development of character or universal virtues, one of which is sincerity, gives life satisfaction and happiness. A talent says something about our genes - what we have inherited. But virtues and developed talents, like sincerity, say something about us. So sincerity will bring you lasting happiness. When you move in the direction of sincerity you are going with nature and this getting in tandem with nature will help you relax and bring you happiness.

The superior man wishes to be slow in his speech & earnest in his conduct.
Virtue is not left to stand alone.
He who practises it will have neighbors.

Why does the superior man wish to be slow in his speech? A superior man does not want to over commit. He does not want to preach something which he cannot practice. He wants to walk his talk. And there is much wisdom in doing what you say, in practicing what you preach and in walking your talk. This makes people trust you. This trust works for you when the chips are down. When your deeds are in tandem with your words, once again, you are in sync with the order of the universe; you are in tune with the Tao. The desire to do what you say also makes you sensible and promising. You will not make false promises. In fact, you may try to under commit and over deliver. Under commit not to avoid the work required to fulfill your intention, but to surprise the other party. This is the reason why the superior man wishes to be slow in his speech and earnest in his conduct.

Confucius goes on to say that virtue is not left to stand alone. He who practices it will have neighbors. The scent of a flower does not go against the wind but the scent of the good does go against the wind. The person of integrity wafts this scent in every direction- the person of integrity does not need the wind to spread his perfume. He himself is a windmill powered by the energy of the universe. His vibe of virtue works like a magnet. That is, other virtuous people catch this vibe and gather around him.

Those who are next to being most sincere person
are those who strive to be sincere.
They start from their actions & words to be sincere.
Once they attain sincerity, their sincerity expresses itself outwardly.
Their expressions will be seen by all & will be even more sincere.
This sincerity will move others thus they can make others change.

Confucius is talking about those who wear the mask of sincerity - They are striving to be sincere. Why does he consider these people next to the best?
These pretenders are just next to the best because he knows that very soon the mask will become the face. Their actions and words will begin to be sincere. That means, sincerity is not coming from the centre to the periphery, it is moving from the periphery to the centre.

But once they attain sincerity, their sincerity expresses itself outwardly and their expressions will be seen by all and will be even more sincere. Their expression will be seen by all. Why? Because a non-sincere person striving to be sincere is news; it makes people notice. A sincere person living sincerely is not news. The new converts make news because they are wearing new clothes, they are changing themselves and that's news - it will broadcast. ...and will be even more sincere, even more sincere than who? Even more sincere than the already sincere people because they are the new converts; they take their religion more seriously. Their sincerity will be such that it makes others move towards change. Others will be moved because they see the swelling ranks of the sincere; they might be moved to become like them thinking that if so many people are converting to the sincere world view there must indeed be something in it.

The most sincere person can foretell the future.
When the state is going to be prosperous there will be a good omen,
when the state is going to be conquered there will be a bad omen.
Fortunes, whether good or bad, can be foretold,
hence the most sincere person is like a God.

Why can the most sincere person foretell the future? Because the hangover of sincerity is a state of poise, deep poise. When you behave sincerely, you come to a state of deep poise. This state of poise will help you access two kinds of intuitions. Let us call the first, grey intuition. Grey Intuition is intuiting through archives stored in your brain. That means this intuition comes from the files stored in your brain. They might be at the conscious or the subconscious level. Sometimes, this kind of intuition wells up so imperceptibly that you wonder where it came from - it is coming from files stored in your library (archives). This kind of intuition goes up with age and is seen very often in professions where the stakes are very high or where life is at stake. For example, in the nursing profession, among firemen; this kind of intuition is very strong. It becomes more easily accessible to you when you are in a state of poise. Most intuition is grey intuition.

There is another type of intuition also which this state of poise will help you access, and that is blue intuition. Blue intuition is intuiting by accessing information from the universal intelligence. From what Carl Jung called collective consciousness of man. You are in sync with the universe and you become a channel for the wisdom of the universe. This type of intuition is rare.

Although, most intuition is grey, a sincere person, in his state of poise can also access blue intuition. Hence, the sincere person is like a God. Confucius really values sincerity. A sincere person is like a deity for him. And as we go further we will realize how a sincere outlook is born and how important it is for the well being of the society.

A superior man maintains a sense of shame.
Shame is the shadow of sincerity.
Sincerity means loyalty.
When you are disloyal, you are ashamed.
Sincerity means integrity.
When you are low on integrity you are ashamed.
Sincerity means honesty.
Honesty means courage, when you are a coward;
when you are dishonest, you are ashamed.

While we are talking about Confucius' stress on sincerity it would be appropriate also to study what he has said about shame.

Why does Confucius say that it is important to maintain a sense of shame?

Is shame good or is shame bad?

As per Confucius shame is good. Today western Psychology agrees with him - shame is good, because shame develops you. When we feel shame we feel distress, embarrassment or anger. It is the place where we learn to stop struggling with ourselves. However, when we dwell in the space of shame, then we grow. Shame is a dark place and we grow by shining a light on the mind's dark places. The dark space of shame is a nursery for human character. It is like the womb. The womb is dark so is the space of shame.

You feel ashamed if, for example, you have behaved cowardly. Then you resolve that next time onward, you will not be a coward. Where is this resolution made? This resolution is made in the soil of shame, so shame develops you and that is why Confucius highlights the importance of shame.

All in all, Confucius is a great votary of sincerity and he feels that a sincere person will be successful. This is also because modern society is glued together with trust. Trust comes from sincere behavior. Whoever can be trusted more will have more partners. People like to collaborate with him, to deal with him. Confucius' understanding has proven right, time and again. Even Max Weber, the great European sociologist, has said that it was the sheer dependability of the protestant businessmen which made them succeed like anything; because they were trust worthy, their businesses boomed. Confucian ethics have come true again and again as the civilization progressed and the first pillar of Confucian ethics is sincerity.

When good government prevails in a state, to be thinking of only salary & when bad government prevails to be thinking in the same way only of salary - this is shameful.

Here Confucius warns you against your covetous instinct, against your greed. He says when the government is good, or when the employer is good, to be thinking only of salary is shameful

.

Who is a good employer?

Firstly, a good employer has a good objective in his business. It might be profit, but it is profit with principles; not just profit. Secondly, a good employer is also loyal. He not only expects loyalty from employees, he too is loyal to his employees. A good employer knows that people don't begin as loyal employees. They observe the employer. When they find the employer trustworthy they become loyal.

So when the government or the employer is good, to be thinking only of salary is shameful. Also, if you are thinking only of salary, then the employer will get to know about this thought of yours, this obsession of yours. And you will lose your place in his heart. You might also lose, if you move away from him or go to another employer who can pay you better. This often proves to your disadvantage in the long run.

In the same way, he says, when bad government prevails to be thinking in the same way only of salary - this is shameful. That means, when the government is bad or the employer is bad then you are just tied with him because he can pay you a good salary. It speaks poorly of you. You become party to not very upright objectives. It is apparent that you are traveling with crooked people just because you are thinking only of salary or that this bad employer can pay you the salary you require, you want. Therefore, this is also shameful and unwise, as many a time in such journeys there is catastrophe ahead.

The practice of perfect virtue is for man himself as well as for others.

Here Confucius is saying that character (perfect virtue) helps man as well as helps others. We have to first understand how character is born. Character is born out of the unique interplay between two opposing forces - the need for personal aggrandizement and the need for a feeling of togetherness. When these two opposing forces, the need for personal aggrandizement and the concern for the other, interplay, character is born. This implies that if character is born because of the interplay of man's selfishness and concern for society, then character should benefit the self interest of the individual as well as the society.

How does character help an individual's self interest?

Firstly, as mentioned before, the development of character brings happiness. Western research has come to this conclusion that when you develop your virtues, you feel satisfied and happy. This one way how character helps the man who is following the path of virtue. There is another way. The world is moving from competition to collaboration. When the world is moving from competition to collaboration, one should first ask this question - Who would you like to collaborate with? Would you like to collaborate with a person who is shady or you would like to collaborate with a person who is straight and virtuous. Naturally, you would like to collaborate with a person who is virtuous. So the man with character will have any takers, because the man with character has credibility. Credibility is his passport to collaborations. And his credibility and virtues help him.

Such a person also helps the society because virtuous conduct promotes social wellbeing and harmony. Through his virtuous acts he uplifts the society and he also uplifts himself. Once Golda Meir, the Prime Minister of Israel was asked, "You were just a school teacher and you became the Prime Minister of Israel and Israel was not such a strong nation state before. But after you took over you made it so powerful. Tell us how you managed both these things?" She replied, there is a plaque on my table which says, ***If I am not for myself, who will be for me? And if I am only for myself what am I?*** So as I knew that nobody would be for me if I am not to be for myself, I lifted myself to become the Prime Minister of Israel. And because I was for others also, because I knew if I am only for myself what am I, I lifted Israel as well and made it one of the most powerful nation states of the world.

Fish, though lying deep in water are visible from above.

Confucius is speaking to the gentleman. And he is telling him that though you may think that you are not visible to others, still they are watching you. So set strict demands on yourself even when you are alone. Even when you are alone, do not do things which you cannot talk about publicly or which you would not like the public to know. This is because you may be like a fish lying deep in water, but people can see you. Someone is watching your living room. So even in the privacy of your living room, live correctly.

Furthermore, in order to have a clear conscience before God, you must follow good conduct. You should live so that you can sell your parrot to the town gossipers.

The man who in the view of gain thinks of righteousness,
who in the view of danger is prepared to give up his life &
who does not forget an old agreement, however far back it extends;
such a man may be reckoned a complete man.

Confucius reiterates that it is not just good enough to be righteous; you should be righteous even in the face of the greatest temptation. You should be prepared to give up your life for your principles, not only in times of peace but also in full view of danger. And just because an agreement is very old you should not back track on it. That is no matter how much dust it might have gathered, if you have agreed to something you stay true to it, you abide by it. Such a man may be reckoned a complete man.

Confucius has deep admiration in his heart for a man who sacrifices profit for principles. In his eyes, a man who sacrifices gain for righteousness is a very intelligent man. Because Confucius feels that when you live with good values brick by brick you construct a temple through your good conduct; by the time it is ready you realize it is also a castle, it has made you impregnable. The robe has become the armour. Confucius feels that this is the way to heaven - the way to peace and happiness.

He who exercises government by means of his virtue
may be compared to the North Pole Star
which keeps its place & all the stars turn towards it.

Here Confucius is saying that just a few people are born with an unwavering compass. Most are born as if they are dry leaves in the breeze - without any direction.

The virtuous people have an unwavering compass inbuilt in them and slowly the others start turning towards them. That is why such people make legends. The legends of the world form around virtuous people. Virtuous people are known to be legendary because everyone follows their trajectory. This is emulated in the universe where all the stars turn towards the North Pole star which is steady in its course.

The book of songs said,
I cherish the memory of a man with virtues,
though he gives me no command or shows us no tender feelings.

Confucius said it is the least important thing to move people with commands and tender feelings (manipulations).

There are two types of people who exploit you - one is the intimidators, they command you. And the other, the manipulators they cajole you. Both these types of people are not welcome. You feel uncomfortable when they are around.

The manipulator is scheming. His path is circuitous. He poses to be what he is not. He is a wolf masquerading as the sheep. He is a friendly thief; he will rob you but many of his victims will never realize that they have been robbed. The second type is the intimidator, who uses force to make you prostate. He commands.

We neither like to be commanded like that nor do we like to be manipulated by tender feelings and therefore Confucius says, that it is the least important thing to move people with commands and tender feelings. He does not approve of it. When we try to control people through tender feelings we play poor me or aloof, try to gain their sympathy, work on their emotions. But the other person is not comfortable - somewhere he understands and deciphers our phoniness; somewhere he understands that we are playing a control drama. He may go with us, but he will not cherish our memory. He will cherish the memory of a person who allows him the feeling of comfort, as well as, wakes him to his own possibilities and urges him to go forward and achieve.

The wise are free from perplexities,
the virtuous from anxiety &
the bold from fear.

Confucius says the wise are free from perplexities, they don't look here and there, and their course is straight in front of them. They will not be in a dilemma. Because they are wise they are the people who have thought things out. They don't have perplexities.

Confucius says that the virtuous are free from anxiety. The virtuous are free from anxiety / worry, but why is the unscrupulous man worried? Because he has done things which he needs to hide. If his deeds come to light, he might get caught and punished.

The bold are free from fear because the shadow of boldness or that of courage is a kind of faith. This faith overpowers fear and defeats it, once and for all. So Confucius says the bold are free from fear because the bold are walking in the shadow of faith.

To cultivate himself, a man must follow the right course.
And to follow the right course,
he must begin with kindness & benevolence.
Being benevolent means to love people.
The greatest benevolence is to love ones own parents.
Justice means to treat things properly.
The greatest justice is to value the wise and virtuous.

Confucius is now talking about how a man can cultivate himself. To cultivate himself, a man must follow the right course - the way of the heaven. And to follow the right course he has to first begin with kindness and benevolence.

Why kindness?

Kindness is the fountain head of many virtues. If we single-mindedly pursue kindness, several other virtues sprout. If we are kind, we will be fair, polite, generous, loving and empathetic. So kindness is the mother of many virtues and that is why Confucius says begin with kindness and then benevolence.

Being benevolent means to love people. The greatest benevolence, he says, is to love one's own parents.

Why is it the greatest benevolence to love one's own parents?

First of all, it is difficult, as there is the grudge of the childhood. Often this grudge surfaces between the son and the father. The father in his thirties, forties and even fifties is very aggressive with the son. He often behaves like a dictator.

His demeanor is of a hot-blooded animal. When the son grows up he starts challenging the authority of the father. Once he is an adult and an independent adult, he would even become antagonistic to the father. So there is the grudge of childhood, which is why often it is difficult to love your parents. Then there is ageism. Just as there is racism in the world, there is ageism in the world. People who grow old, slowly become unwelcome for the society. Though one often draws similarity between the old and an infant - both are dependent on you, but infants are cute, loving and not set in their mindsets like the old. Confucius knows these realities and how difficult it is to love one's own parents. Therefore, he says the greatest love; the highest peak is if you can love your own parents.

He also knows it is very important, even for selfish reasons, to love one's parents.

Pythagoras, the Greek Philosopher, said that if your near and dear relationships are in harmony, then you will perform brilliantly. That is, one should be a good son, tender spouse, just brother and a loyal friend. (Confucius has added to this list - one should be a good ruler or a good subject also). If you are all this, then all your near and dear relationships are in harmony and then when you kick the ball you kick it with a very relaxed and poised state of mind. Then it automatically bends like David Beckham's shot and enters the goal post. Hence, this is another reason why Confucius kept benevolence towards one's own parents as the highest kind of benevolence.

Also he knows that often the way to love your parents is to first forgive your parents. When a child grows into an adult he understands all adults are imperfect. When he grows into a wise adult he forgives them and forgives himself also. Meaning thereby, that the child, as he is growing is harboring certain grudges. As he grows into an adult, he rebels a little then understands all adults are imperfect, then forgives his parents and then forgives himself also for having rebelled against his parents. It is then that he becomes truly wise.

Moreover, a wise man is quick to forgive. He wants you to love your parents because he knows that in trying to love your parents you will pass through the stairs of forgiveness which will also develop you. Forgiveness helps you develop by allowing you to drop the unnecessary baggage of hurt that you are carrying. If you don't forgive your parents you will stay stuck in the past.

Then he says justice means to treat things properly. The greatest justice is to value the wise and virtuous people. Justice means fairness and the greatest justice is to value the wise and virtuous people for two reasons - firstly, wise and virtuous people may often tell you that you are wrong. In such a case, if you are fair yourself, then only you are able to see things in perspective. Secondly, wise and virtuous people often come under attack by slanderous people who spread rumors against them and might even try to poison your ears. You need to have a good sense of justice to continue to be fair to the wise and the virtuous.

The most important relationships in the world are five in number -
ruler & subjects,
father & sons,
husband & wife,
brother and friends.
The maintenance and improvement of these relationships
depends on three virtues -
wisdom, benevolence and courage.

Wisdom is the ability to understand the long view of things. To see the true nature of things and then make the choices which are true, right and lasting. It is to be informed by the sum of learning through the ages using multiple forms of intelligence: reason, instinct, intuition, heart and spirit. True wisdom is grounded in past experience or history and yet it is able to anticipate the likely consequences in the future. It balances self interest with public good. It helps one work with and aligns oneself to life.

Wisdom will make all these five relationships - Ruler and subjects, father and son, husband and wife, brother and friends - function smoothly. If these relationships work smoothly then society works smoothly. Wisdom is the first grease for these relationships and perhaps, the most important grease for these relationships. The second is benevolence by which he means love; and this also means in some sense kindness and in another sense tolerance. Tolerance is required for society to function smoothly.

And the third lubricant which the society requires so that it functions smoothly is courage. Because he understands that with benevolence, with love, there needs to be discipline. There has to be the courage to take disciplinary action also. Otherwise, human nature is such that it will start taking love for granted.

To be able under all circumstances
to practise these five things constitutes perfect virtue.
These five things are -
gravity, generosity of soul, sincerity, earnestness and kindness.

Confucius knows that if you are dignified you will not be treated with disrespect, so he recommends gravity. He recommends generosity of soul because he knows that if you are generous you will win all. Third, you should be sincere; if you are sincere, people will repose trust in you. Fourth, if you are earnest (determined and passionate) you will accomplish much. Finally, if you are kind it will enable you to employ the services of others; others will come to you and work with you, your cause will gather momentum because of your kindness. This is why he recommends gravity, generosity of soul, sincerity, earnestness and kindness.

There are nine set principles to administer the state:
to cultivate one's moral character,
to value virtuous persons,
to be on intimate terms with relatives,
to esteem high officials,
to understand and sympathize with all officials,
to care about the common people,
to attract all kinds of workers,
to appease those who are far away and
to think of the dukes.

Let us examine the nine principles outlined by Confucius for effective administration of state:

1. To cultivate one's moral character: It is evident Confucius is a great one for character. He feels character is the sin qua non of a personality. For him a man without character is an animal.

2. To value virtuous people: To be able to value virtuous people, the ruler must drive away the slanderers. Also, he should refrain from sensual pleasures. Confucius recommends this because he feels liquor can make you lose your cool, dull your faculties of judgment and you might end up, insulting the virtuous or misbehaving with them.

3. To be on intimate terms with relatives: This was very important for administration during the Confucian time because the clan helped in governing, and maximum jealousy sprouted within the clan only. So when

you became a ruler, the most jealous people were your own family members. Therefore, he says, take them along with you, give them important positions, and raise their ranks and salaries. Wherever they deserve to have a good position, do give it to them. Also try and have the same likes and dislikes. Confucius says that if you don't have the same likes and dislikes as your relatives, after sometime they will bore you or you will bore them.

4. To esteem high officials: The high officials should be given their place in the scheme of things. They should be given respect even by the ruler. Also the ruler should trust his high officials because if a feeling goes to the ranks and staff that the higher official is not trusted, then it becomes very difficult for the higher officials to rule the rank and staff.

5. To understand and sympathize with all officials: To raise their salaries when required.

6. To care about the common people through good governance, infrastructure, reasonable taxes and law and order: For Confucius the welfare of the common man is the most important. Why does he say that the officials should be taken care of? Because he feels that if the officials are happy, the common man will be happy. However, if the officials are happy and not working hard, not working diligently then Confucius' prescription for them is to dismiss them.

7. To attract all kinds of workers: So there should be good labor laws, good working and living conditions and equality of opportunity.

8. To appease those who are far away: Here he talks about the governors, those

who have been appointed by you to handle states in far away lands. They should be kept happy.

9. To think of the dukes: Dukes are kings who have accepted your superiority. But they are in far away lands and they are strong themselves. Confucius advises the ruler to control the strong and protect the weak. To restrain the strong. And save the weak from rebellions under him. If there is rebellion under a duke, the emperor should help him in quelling it. Help the dukes when they are in trouble. Keep contact with them. Plus restrain them. Confucius feels that if you think of the dukes you will be able to control them. Because if you keep thinking of them then you will find ways to find out what is happening in their dukedoms. Also, whenever things are getting out of hand or going against your national interest you will be able to correct them.

When a prince's personal conduct is correct,
his government is efficient without the issuing of orders.
If his personal conduct is not correct,
he may issue orders but they will not be followed.

Here Confucius advises the ruler that he should align his video with his audio. That means whatever he says, he should do; only then, his command will be followed. At another place he has said,

If you lead on the people with correctness, who will dare not be correct.
If you are not covetous although, you reward them to steal they would not do so.

That means, the habit of stealing in the public is taken from the king. This virus spreads from the top. The top sets the agenda. If the king were to steal an apple from the orchard, the public would uproot the orchard - it would steal everything. This is what happened in India and many other countries which were governed by the British. The British stole from these colonies. Since they were the government, the kings, the public caught on and they started stealing too. For this reason, for many years, even after the British left these countries, public property was stolen right, left and centre. It continued to be stolen; whether it was toilet paper in the toilets or it was mugs from the railway compartments or even soaps in the toilets of railway compartments. It is only now and that too slowly, that public property is beginning to be respected in these countries.

Confucius also says,

Employ the upright and put aside all the crooked.
In this way the crooked can be made upright.

If you punish the crooked and reward the upright, more and more people will turn towards uprightness. Having said that, he says, *pardon small faults and raise to office a man of virtue and talents*. To begin with, pardon small faults, so that you allow people time to change. When you come as a new ruler you cannot immediately ask people to change and punish severely for small faults. Pardon small faults, ignore them. You are setting the culture for them. And raise to office a man of virtue and talents - everybody will look up to him and they will follow him. Slowly more and more will begin to follow in this man's footsteps.

The requisites of government are that
there will be sufficiency of food,
of military equipments and
the confidence of the people in their ruler.

The first requisite is evident - sufficiency of food. So a good state should have sufficiency of food. Second is sufficiency of military equipments. That means, not only should a good state have enough to feed everybody, it should be strong enough to defend its interests also. Finally, there must be confidence of the people in their ruler. The ruler should be a man of gravity, of character. This inspires confidence of the people in their ruler so even through a time of adversity, they will not desert him. They will not question his ability to govern.

Like the four seasons, he acted in a timely manner.
Like the sun and the moon he shines brilliantly.
All creations prospered without doing harm to each other.

Here Confucius is describing the attributes of a good ruler. Like the four seasons he acts in a timely manner that means, he is wise enough to gauge the tenor of the times, he can sniff the spirit of the times and then act appropriately. There is a time to move like lightning and there is a time to stand still like a mountain. This ruler knows when it is time for what.

Like the sun and the moon he shines brilliantly - the ruler is a virtuous man and with an excellent reputation. All creations prosper under him without doing harm to each other. He protects the weak and controls the strong. If the strong are left without restraint they will attack, overpower and exploit the weak.

He knew the two extreme ways of governing but preferred to govern the people according to the way of the mean. This is the reason why he possessed great wisdom.

What are the two extreme ways of governing ?

One way suggests that you rule with fear. When people will fear you they will obey you and your rule will continue. Here the handle of the rule is in your hand as long as they fear you. The other, equally extreme way, is to rule through love. Here the leader feels that only as long as he loves his people, they will listen to him and the rule will continue smoothly.

Both the ways are eccentric ways. In the first way, you burn the very energies of the group by continuing to scare them and it also develops resentment in the long run. In the second way, the way of extreme love, you surrender the whip. The whip is, once in a while, required to bring discipline in the organization. You also lose awe. Now it depends on the people - if they are good people, they will obey you but even when they are obeying you, you have lost your awe.

So what is the preferred way of governing - Confucius preferred to govern the people according to the way of the mean. The way of the mean is where you love also and at the same time you discipline as well. Love and discipline go hand in hand. Too much love will spoil your people. They will eventually hurt themselves. Too much fear will make them resentful or will sap their initiative. The right way is to govern with love and discipline and the discipline should be of the variety which tells everybody that the person who is being disciplined is not being disciplined for harassment. The purpose of the discipline is to reform him.

Thereafter he goes to say, *Chu is retiring, therefore I urge him forward. Yu has more than his share of energy therefore I keep him back.* What he means is, you need to have different strokes for different folks. One of his people, Chu is retiring and slow, therefore, he has to be pushed from time to time. And Yu has more than his share of energy. Sometimes he may err because of his haste, because of his passion. So he keeps him back. Again this is also the way of the mean.

What is meant by the four bad things -
to put people to death without having instructed them,
this is called cruelty;
to require from them suddenly the full trial of work
without having given them warning this is called oppression;
to issue orders as if without urgency at first and
when the time comes to insist on them with severity, this is called injury
and generally in giving pay or rewards to men to do so in a stingy way
this is called acting the part of a petty official.

Confucius is stressing that the ruler should be reasonable. Only when people have been instructed adequately, when the culture is set, then punishment should be given. Without training, people should not be suddenly loaded with important tasks and if this is the way to train, then small faults should be overlooked. Also when you are issuing orders, if you are issuing them without urgency at first then you should not insist on them with severity suddenly. Because doing so is an injury to the system. And when you are paying rewards, that time you should not be stingy. You should not act in a way which is petty.

I would not seek praise from posterity
by advocating eccentric theories and behaving treacherously.
A gentleman should follow the way of the mean and
I will not give it up half way even if others do so.
A gentleman should stay in the mean and
should not have regrets even if he remains unknown to others.
Only a sage can adhere to these principles.

Confucius knows that the mean does not startle. Mean is the middle. When you are in the middle, it is not startling. When you are in the extreme then it is startling. So he says, *I will not seek praise from posterity by advocating such extreme theories*. First of all, I will not advocate extreme theories. Secondly, I am also almost *immune to praise from posterity*. By praise from posterity, he means fame. Confucius understands that fame is like the dust cloud which follows your car when you are going from point A to point B, which is your destination. The important thing is to reach the destination; it's not how much dust you gather and how many people notice you. A gentleman is not smitten by fame.

The point is to reach destination B. Confucius also knows that when one pursues fame his happiness now lies in what others are thinking of him i.e. his happiness lies in other people's heads! So he tells you not to bother about fame.

Then he goes on to say that *a gentleman should follow the way of the mean and I will not give it up half way even if others do so*. Even if others do not follow the way of the mean, they behave in extreme ways, still I will decide how I need to respond to them and my response to them will be in accordance with the way of the mean.

What does Confucius mean by the way of the mean?

It is balance - the balance that a man acquires when he moves on the middle path. When he avoids extremes and follows the golden mean then, for example, he is not a coward nor is he rash he is courageous. Similarly, between pride and diffidence he chooses modesty, between miserliness and extravagance he chooses liberality, between depression and buffoonery he chooses good humor, between belligerence and flattery he chooses friendship. This balance is what Confucius is talking about - not being too much here nor being too much there.

There is a Hindi couplet which says,

"Sambhal jaane do Mira ke thirakti payal,
Aur Gautam ke sadhe paon zara behek jane do"

It speaks of Mira who is frivolous and tells her to sober a little and its speaks of Gautam Buddha who is too serious and it tells him to relax a little. Come in the middle. In Chinese, there is a word called Zhong Yong - which says, in the middle and in equilibrium. This is what Confucius means when he says that one should follow the way of the mean.

Then he goes on to say, a gentlemen should stay in the mean and have no regrets even if he remains unknown to others. Confucius knows that fame does provide some satisfaction. At the same time he also knows, what are the side-effects of fame. One of the important side-effects of fame is that, once your picture forms in the mind of another man(that is fame); then you are constrained to live just in accordance with that picture. It restricts your freedom. So he knows about the side-effect of fame and he knows that even if he does not get fame, he will not subscribe to extreme theories.

When he says, only a sage can adhere to the principle of the mean, he is speaking in the long-term. In the long-term, it is difficult to be always in the mean. You keep falling off on either sides.

He with whom,
neither slander that gradually soaks into the mind
nor statements that startle,
cause the wound in the flesh are successful,
may be called intelligent indeed.

Confucius is now referring to equanimity. To keep one's own counsel and equanimity. He is saying that slander (when somebody criticizes and spreads rumors about somebody else) soaks gradually into the mind, first time you might deny it as a canard, then you think about it, you ruminate on it and slowly it starts soaking into your mind. He says that a true man will not allow this to happen. He is impervious to slander.

Nor statements that startle can cause a wound in the flesh... statements which are harsh and directed against you and which can scar an ordinary man, such statements also do not startle or scare this complete man - then he is really intelligent.

A man in a superior situation,
having valour without righteousness, will be guilty of insubordination.
One of lower people having valour without righteousness
will commit robbery.

Confucius here highlights balancing traits (He is still talking about the way of the mean). A man in a superior situation, who is courageous but not righteous, will be guilty of insubordination. Because he does not know what norms to follow, he just has his boldness to back him. So he could become guilty of insubordination.

Similarly, a man among the subordinate staff who has boldness but is not righteous, does not have character, can commit robbery. Therefore, the balancing virtue is important - Boldness is balanced with righteousness. Then, you can take command and you will not misuse the power which boldness gives you.

I hate those who are only not modest and think that they are valourized.
I hate those who make known secrets and think they are straight- forward.
Of all people, girls and servants are the most difficult to behave to.
If you are familiar with them, they lose their humility,
if you maintain a reserve towards them, they are discontented.

Confucius points out how the talk of balance can be misinterpreted or how when you are prescribing a particular attribute, the person who is your student or who is your audience, might mistake it for something else which he has, and without changing himself, start labeling himself as virtuous. How someone who is not modest, may think he is brave or bold; someone who cannot keep secrets may think that he is straight-forward. Such people who live in such illusions of virtue, masquerade, unknowingly, their weaknesses as their virtue.

And then Confucius says - of all people, girls and servants are the most difficult to deal with. Girls are emotional, servants are uneducated. In this reference, he says that if you are familiar with them, they lose their humility - that means, if you are friendly with them, they will cross the line between you and them. They will forget their position in the overall scheme of things in the organization. And if you maintain reserve towards them they are discontented and they may take you as arrogant.

The way of the mean is not beyond our reach.
Some think it is not worth practising because
it is too near to us and seek something far and difficult to do.
This is not the way of the mean.

Confucius asks why are we not challenged by the mean?

Because the mean seems too near. Whatever is near and within reach does not challenge our ego. Our ego wants to do something difficult - climb the highest mountain, swim the widest sea and so on. (Confucius also knows that the mean is not difficult to get at. What is difficult is to stay there.)

*Book of Songs said, cut the handle of a new axe with an old axe and
it will not be far from the old handle in appearance.
Hence a gentleman asks of others no more than of himself,
so long as they correct their mistakes.
He who can practise tolerance and forbearance
is not far from the way of the mean.
He should do to others as he would have others do to him.*

Confucius highlights now the severity of the challenge of the mean. *Cut the handle of a new axe with an old axe and it will not be far from the old handle in appearance.* Even though you decide to change, the new will take time to settle. In the beginning, the new will still resemble the old because it is the inertia of the old which will hold you.

Hence a gentleman asks of others no more than of himself so long as they correct their mistakes. Here he is telling of the practical difficulty of following the way of the mean. Following the way of the mean is as if walking on that single rail track that we used to as children. You have to balance yourself. You walk a distance and then your step falls either on the right or on the left of the track and you are off balance. Then you come back again. So the way of the mean is like falling again and again on either side and coming back again. Erring again and again but less and less and less. That's the way of the mean.

Hence the gentlemen asks of others no more than of himself so long as they correct their mistakes. He knows he himself cannot keep on the way of the mean for long. So as long as people come back on the way of the mean after going left or right, he is okay with it. Because he, himself does that.

He who can practice tolerance and forbearance is not far from the way of the mean.

And then Confucius said, **(five centuries before Christ)** *he should do onto others as he would have others do onto him.* He says that just as I forgive myself from going astray, I will forgive others also.

There are four ways to be a gentleman
but I am unable to follow any of them -
I cannot wait upon my father as I ask of my son,
I cannot serve my lord as I ask of my subordinates,
I cannot respect my elder brother as I ask of my younger brother,
I cannot treat my friends as I ask my friends to treat me.

Here again, Confucius shares his humanness, his vulnerability. He exposes his own vulnerability by saying I cannot serve my father as much as I expect my son to serve me, I cannot serve my superior as much as I want my subordinates to serve me, I cannot respect my elder brother as much as I ask my younger brother to respect me and I cannot treat my friends as I ask them to treat me. So he is aware of this little difference in the frequencies of his expectations and his performance. And this awareness will bring his performance in line with his expectations. When he will speak, he will think of his acts, when he expects he will think of his own delivery, when he acts he will remember what he has said - then he will reach the next level of evolution.

What qualities a man must possess to entitle him to be a scholar?
He must be earnest, urgent and bland -
Among his friends earnest and urgent,
among his brethren bland.

Why is Confucius saying that if you wish to be a scholar, among your friends you should be earnest and urgent?

Earnest means determined, dedicated, so that your friends know that you have a cause to attend to and allow you the freedom to do so. And urgent meaning that he should not loiter around. He should quickly dispose off his interactions with his friends. He should not be a time waster, he should be quick.

But among his brethren he should be bland. Confucius is suggesting that you be bland among your family if you wish to be a scholar. By bland, he means boring. Why is he suggesting that one should be boring among his family if he wishes to be scholar? Because friends are more understanding and they will give you the space, but sometimes with family, particularly in the eastern part of the world- when you are with elderly people in the family - you have to give them your time; even if you feel that the time is not being used productively. So he has suggested that you be boring among your family. By family he means your cousins, your brothers, sisters - be a bit boring there. Do your duty but be a bit boring so that they allow you the space to continue your study. When they find you boring, they wish to get rid of you, then you can go back to your library or study.

In fact he also said that in a village of ten families you might find one person as sincere as I am but you will not find anybody as fond of learning as I am. Confucius is of the view that even if you have to be carrying a pretence to be boring, it is okay because your objective is good. This little chicanery is permitted.

A scholar in his eager pursuit of knowledge forgets his food.
In the joy of its attainment, forgets his sorrows and
does not perceive that old age is coming.

Confucius defines the attributes of a scholar. So eager he is about learning that he forgets his food. His passion for learning so consumes him that he doesn't even remember the need of his body for food. In Greece, it is said that Plato was so fond of reading that in the night when it was time to sleep and his senses were giving way, his eyes were closing and his body was tired, he used to hold the book he was reading in one hand and he used to hold a metal ball in the other hand. And just beneath the hand with the ball, on the floor, he kept a metal pan. So he knew that if he went off to sleep while reading the book, his hand would drop and the ball would hit the metal pan below. The clanging noise would wake him up again. Then Plato would resume his learning again - with his book in one hand and the metal ball in the other.

In his eager pursuit of knowledge and in the joy of his attainments, he forgets his sorrows. When you learn something you grow. This growth gives you pleasure. It is like a mental orgasm. And this orgasm makes you forget your sorrows. And one does not even perceive that old age is coming. One of the best remedies to slow down the onset of old age is to be in a learning mode, have the proverbial school bag always on your shoulder. Because when one is in that learning mode - in a student mode - the student mode takes him mentally to that school boy kind-of-state and youthful juices start flowing. That is why one does not perceive that old age is coming.

Confucius also feels that the love of learning helps you balance the pursuit of virtues because he knows that virtue when taken to an extreme can start becoming counter productive. In Chinese, there is a phrase *Wu Ji Bi Fan* which means, that once something reaches its extreme, it will start turning to the other direction. This direction could be a negative direction also. The opposite of what it is will start being born in it. He knows that for example:

Benevolence, if taken to an extreme without the love of learning would lead to foolish simplicity.
Straight-forwardness without the love of learning will lead to rudeness.
Love of boldness without the love of learning will lead to insubordination.
Love of firmness without the love of learning will result in extreme conduct.
Love of being sincere without the love of learning will develop an injurious disregard of consequences.

Learning is the governor. It will control the virtue so that it doesn't go berserk. So Confucius is for learning because he knows that such learning will enable the virtuous man to stay on-track. Otherwise, blind pursuit of virtue can lead to disaster.

The superior ruler is
one who maintains a dignified ease without being proud,
one who is majestic without being fierce and
one who is beneficent without great expenditure.

Confucius again counsels balance; balance in ruling. When a ruler is dignified without being proud, the other people around him are comfortable and at the same time they do not encroach on the perimeter of dignified space which the ruler needs, to govern. He maintains a dignified ease. Not only is he dignified, he is also relaxed.

One who is majestic without being fierce - there is majesty in him. At the same time there is not the harshness of a dictator, there is not the stridency of a tyrant; there is a majesty, which is not too loud, which is not acerbic.

Also a ruler is one who is *beneficent without great expenditure* - what does this mean? Beneficent (kind and generous) without great expenditure? But how is this possible? Imagine, you are the boss and an agitated employee comes to you and vents steam. He is angry about something, he hollers about it and then he goes. You just listen to him. You have neither cajoled him nor have you reprimanded him, you have just listened to him. He has vented steam. He might go back home and tell his wife that today he said his piece and that he is happy about it. He is feeling brave. Your silent demeanor allowed him to be a hero for sometime. Your silent demeanor allowed him to once again know that he is free to speak, free to say his piece. This itself brings satisfaction in the job. If his grievance has been received by a mature variety of silence it doesn't hurt your authority. Once in a while, you can give your shoulder for people to cry on. They feel a greater sense of belongingness. This is one example of being beneficent without great expenditure.

There are three principles of conduct
which the man of high rank should consider especially important.
That in his deportment and manner
he keeps from violence and heedlessness.
That in regulating his countenance he keeps near to sincerity
and in his words and tones he keeps far from lowness and impropriety.

That in his deportment (conduct and manner) he keeps away from violence and heedlessness. There should be a digestive system which should be available to the man of power. This digestive system helps him digest his success and his power. When this happens, then he will not misuse his power. Then for a small wrong, just because he is more powerful, he will not go and bludgeon the enemy or the violator. There will be restraint which will come in his behaviour out of kindness towards those that he is ruling. Also he would understand that even when one is much more powerful than the other, violence is not always the best way. Often your power will continue only if you have been able to keep your instinct for violence under check. He is neither heedless nor a rash person - he is a balanced person. He will not suddenly rush in to a decision without thinking of the consequences. Even when there is an instinct in him to get angry, he will think of the consequences.

That in regulating his countenance he keeps near to sincerity - regulating his countenance means, when he is chiseling his image (every ruler or high official chisels his image - he knows how he wants others to see him and he tries to paint a picture of himself as per this wish) he should keep near to sincerity. Meaning, how he wants people to perceive him, should not be far from what he is. It should be as close as possible. Then he is living close to his surface and then this image will endure. Otherwise, after a couple of years or after sometime people will discover that there is a big gap in what he wants to be known as and what he is actually and then he will fall from grace. There is another reason why Confucius says that his image should be sincere, should be close to reality it is because he knows the problem with fame. One of the problems with fame is that you start depending on what the other person thinks of you. And often you start behaving according to his image of you. He knows that fame or an exaggerated image of yourself in another's mind is something which will lead you to distress. This is because, then you become like a puppet in another's hands. It's not a great thing to be having the source of your happiness in other people's heads. That means, your whole life's center of gravity shifts towards the other person's mind. So your image should be close to your reality.

Next Confucius says and in his words and tones he keeps far from brazenness and impropriety. He says that the man of high rank uses his words with care. He knows when to be respectful, when to be friendly and when to be authoritarian. He uses his words in the right measure. He does not use slang, his words are proper and so is his tone, carefully selected. In sum, essentially, good words, delivered in a good tone.

The way a gentleman practises the mean course
is the same as walking a long distance.
He must begin from where he stands.
It's like climbing a high mountain.
He must start from the low places.

Confucius is trying to tell us that the way of the mean, the middle way, is a marathon. It's a mountain to be climbed. So how do you start, from where you start - you must begin from where you are standing. When you are at the bottom of the mountain, you look at the mountain and you begin from wherever you are. Confucius knows it is difficult to begin. There are two problems with starting / beginning - when the task is very big in front of us, we don't look at the first step, we look at the entire staircase and we are numbed into paralysis. Which is why, Goethe says that *boldness has genius in it* - Whatever you want to do, begin boldly. He stresses on the beginning because he knows that once you begin it, you will ultimately reach the end also. We spend a lot of time in the beginning. Confucius is saying, start from the low places, start from wherever you are. The other reason why we find it difficult to begin a thing is because of the inertia of not doing it. To start something from scratch is difficult. You are scared. Which is why, authors often finish their work for a day in mid sentence. That means they don't finish the last sentence of the day. They leave it mid sentence, so next morning, because half of the sentence has already been framed the day before, it provides them some kind of momentum. It works against this inertia to start and they can more easily start the next day.

Miro was a great painter. He had a great gift for aesthetics as well as for imagination. But after a few years in his profession, he hit a road block. What was the road block? The moment he used to stand in front of the canvas, he used to feel numb. He could not lift the brush and draw even the first line. So what did he do? He discovered the Miro star, which is the star you make with a collection of a few triangles. You would have done it as a child. It resembles the asterisk on your keyboard. Without looking at the canvas, he used to draw the Miro's star on the canvas. It was easy to draw. Just a notation, may be a few stars and that used to give him the momentum and then he would draw the whole picture. And his Miro star peeped from behind that picture. All his pictures have a Miro star.

This is why Confucius encourages you to just start. Don't worry about the peak; start on the path. Don't look at the peak - look at the first step on the path.

If a good man were to govern a country in succession for 100 years he would be able to transform the country.

100 is just a figure which Confucius has used. He means for a long tenure. If a good man is at the helm of affairs for a long tenure, he would be able to transform the country. By good man he means, a wise ruler.

Give a wise ruler enough time and he will change the face of the nation. These words came true again and again. Countries which did not go for democracy, countries where one person ruled with an iron hand, but he was a well-meaning person, in those countries too these words came true. Let us take the example of Singapore. Lee Kuan Yew who ruled Singapore from 1959 to 1990, was a well-meaning, wise ruler. He handled all the crises which the country faced because of its neighbors, particularly Malaysia. He handled the dilapidated infrastructure and raised a new one. He handled the great problem posed because of lack of land and an uneducated population and took Singapore to where it is today. Something similar is happening in China - Mao ruled China and now, the fruits of that rule the whole world will be seeing. He might have been a hard handed ruler but he ruled it in a similar, well-meaning way. Particularly for disadvantaged countries, uneducated countries, of Asia, Africa or Latin America it is better to be ruled by one person who is well-meaning and wise, than to spring up inefficient and corrupt politicians every 5 years through the process of elections. When a country is poor and backward, it could be better that a well meaning benevolent autocrat comes to power and stays in power. He could just take it out of its decadence much sooner.

When a public is not fortunate enough to get such a ruler and it is saddled with inefficient and corrupt government (as we have in India) then, it should at every poll defeat the incumbent governments till its message is delivered unequivocally.

The book of songs says
cover satin clothes with cotton overalls.

This is because satin is too showy and the way of a gentleman is to conceal his virtues without showing off. In the end the virtues will indeed emerge. On the other hand, the way of a petty person is to show off, but in the end, the public realizes there was more showbiz, there wasn't enough content or the image was much better than the reality. Confucius wants a person to keep a low profile. He knows if he shows off his satin, whether it is his riches or his virtues and so on, there will be jealousy. And the jealous could either sabotage his achievements or write them off as being due to a stroke of luck or even some dishonest deeds. So the satin's sheen will irritate the other people's eyes and they will become jealous. That is why you should not show off. *Cover satin clothes with cotton.*

In fact, Confucius is of the view, that a leader should not show his riches, otherwise those who are with him or who are his associates, their expectations from him will also increase. In fact, Confucius would like you to fly below the radar till you are so far gone that even when the jealous do spot you, you are outside their firing range.

Here it is important to understand that Confucius also feels that extravagance leads to insubordination. When you pay your people too well then they can become complacent. This complacency is also a precursor to insubordination. Because then they are not good enough to be subordinates and secondly, they might actually become difficult to rule. So in every sense he is advising to keep a low profile.

The stern dignity of antiquity showed itself in grave reserve.
The stern dignity of the present day
shows itself in quarrelsome perverseness.
The stupidity of antiquity showed itself in straightforwardness,
the stupidity of the present shows itself in sheer deceit.

Here Confucius is talking not of two ages but of two generations. He is speaking about the past and the present generation, the last and the current generation. He says *the stern dignity of antiquity showed itself in grave reserve* - the elderly were too serious and there was a lot of stress on dignity. Now the situation has taken a complete 180 degree turn. Now the younger generation takes it to the other extreme and fights with the older generation equally and ferociously, *quarrelsome perverseness* - defiance. So from too much formality and hierarchy we are coming to a stage of defiance. Both these extremes in the Confucian paradigm, are incorrect and unwise.

The stupidity of antiquity showed itself in straight forwardness. Here he says that the principled people of past generations were too straight forward and not worldly-wise.

The *Rajput* kings were valiant fighters. Will Durant has compared them to Charlemagne and King Arthur. Still they lost their empires. One of the chief reasons why *Rajputs* lost their kingdoms and their people were enslaved was because they didn't know that to conquer evil, you have to once in a while enter evil. Krishna has said it in the East. Machiavelli has said it in the West. The good man should have the courage to enter evil.

The Rajputs had principles like not fighting post Sun set. The Mughal invaders knew that the Rajputs will stick to their principles and so attacked them often during night time thus facing hardly any resistance. It was the duty of the Rajput kings to side step the principle and retaliate ferociously against such attacks. When they didn't it cost them their kingdoms and cost their people their freedom. One's principles should exalt him and not straitjacket him. The good side should win. When the good side loses it is the worst advertisement for the cause of goodness. We lost our freedom because of such unwise leaders. They did not know when to make an exception.

The stupidity of the present day shows itself in sheer deceit. Today people have moved to the other side, the other end of the spectrum. They have no principles. Confucius is totally against this breed.

To be poor without murmuring is difficult;
to be rich without being proud is easier.

Here Confucius says that it is easier to be rich without being proud. As when you are rich, you feel fortunate. You are at ease with yourself; you may also feel compassionate towards those people who are not as fortunate as you are. All rich people do realize that there is some role which luck has played in bringing them their fortune. They also realize that pride may bring a fall.

For all these reasons, it is much easier to be rich without being proud, than it is to be poor without murmuring. When you are poor, a murmur is more natural. Because when you are poor, then the necessities of life which you don't have make you uncomfortable. Your family also might make you uncomfortable that you are not being able to provide enough for them. The imprudent sections of the rich community also might make you uncomfortable by not giving you your due in the society. They are judging you only by what you have and not what you are. Therefore, it is more difficult to be poor without murmuring.

Zekun said,
What you pronounce concerning
the poor man who yet does not flatter and
the rich man who is not proud.
The master replied,
They will do but they are not equal to him who though poor is yet cheerful
and to him who though rich, loves the rule of propriety.

The poor man who does not flatter, means the man who's self-respecting and he does not nurse nor pander to the rich man's ego by flattering him. And the rich man who is not proud - he does not pander to his own ego. Just because he is rich he doesn't feel that he is bigger or greater than the ones who are poor. These people are good as per the master but they are not equal to the one who though poor is yet cheerful.

Here Confucius has taken it beyond ego. He admires that man who is poor and still he is happy. So he is saying that there is a greater achievement than bringing your ego to ease and that it is bringing your soul to ease. Since his soul is at ease he is cheerful. And similarly, he says I admire that rich man who though rich, loves the rules of propriety. Though he is rich, this richness has not gone to his head; his wallet is swollen not his head. He loves virtue and propriety.

There are three things which a superior man guards against.
In youth, when the physical powers are not yet settled;
he guards against lust.
When he is strong and physical powers are full of vigor;
he guards against quarrelsomeness.
When he is old and the animal powers are decadent;
he guards against covetousness.

Here, Confucius is talking about protecting people from themselves. He is talking about building dams so that the river of life does not flood. He is talking about 3 stages in a man's life, what kind of dams should he build and what kind of restrain he should show in each of these stages.

- In youth when the physical powers are not yet settled; he guards against lust. Because, the lust is strong and testosterone is surging. He guards against lust so that he does not go astray.

- When he is strong and physical powers are in full vigour; he guards against quarrelsomeness, lest, he wound others or set up deep retaliation. He guards against violence, he guards against heedlessness and rash behavior because the physical powers are full of vigour. Even with his family members, his wife, son and others, he is restrained. Because of his physical superiority nobody can stand in front of him. He has to protect himself from these physical powers getting the better of him and harming others, as well as, him.

- When he is old and the animal powers are decadent; he guards against covetousness. Once animal powers are gone, one should not be greedy, one should be detached. Because, if one is not detached then, mentally he will be upset when he doesn't see things happening his way. This will create some kind of a disease in him. A state of unease. And if one still tries to be greedy, his efforts will be curtailed or they will be in vain. Because he doesn't have the animal powers and he is not strong enough any more.

There is a beautiful gem here;
should I lay it up in a case and keep it or
should I seek for a good price and sell it?
Sell it! Sell it!
But wait for one to offer the price.

Here, Confucius is talking about delayed gratification. Imagine, a child about 3 yrs of age is offered Rs 10,000/- or a box of chocolates, he would go for the box of chocolates. Because he is not wise enough to understand that these Rs 10,000/- can get him chocolates for many days together. He does not know how to delay gratification. He wants immediate pleasure, immediate compensation. In this verse, this is what Confucius is asking to guard against.

Where the student is saying that I found a beautiful gem and should I preserve it or should I seek a good price for it? Confucius says, seek a good price for it but wait for one to offer the price. Wait for the right man who will offer the right price and who will also value the product.

Acorn, (an ancient symbol of abundance), this seed of the mighty Oak tree begins growing only when the tree reaches maturity. This is an allied point. Which means that one has to be patient. Only when the Oak tree will reach maturity, will it be able to sprout an acorn; which can make another mighty oak sprout. So, Confucius is referring to patience here. He is saying - be patient. Hold on to what you have till you find the right customer.

Looked at from a distance he appears stern,
when approached, he appears mild.
When he is heard to speak, his language is firm and decided.

Here, Confucius is referring to the ruler, who looks and should look stern from a distance, so that the people who have evil intentions don't think that he is an easy prey. When approached, he is mild because he takes himself neither too seriously nor frivolously. His path is the path of sobriety, his interactions are polite and yet they are marked with grace. This is why, when he speaks, his language is firm and decided. In short, when he has the courage and countenance of a General and the compassion of a Saint, he is a true ruler.

When agreements are made according to what is right,
what is spoken can be made good.
When respect is shown according to what is proper,
one keeps far from shame and disgrace.

Here Confucius is saying that as long as the agreement stands on what is moral and correct, its spirit can be preserved. In fact, the biggest safeguard in a contract is not in the contract, it is in dealing with the right people and following the right framework. Dealing with the right people and following the right framework will ensure the spirit of the contract is honored and what is orally assured is also made good.

When respect is shown according to what is proper one keeps far from shame and disgrace. Here Confucius has gone a bit deeper where he says that when you over-respect or under-respect a person you feel a sense of shame. You are a little uncomfortable when you have not given respect to someone to whom it was due. At the same time, you feel a little uncomfortable when you have given respect, more than what was required. It can be problematic in the future. This happens very often in eastern society, especially, when eastern people interact with western people. In the East, elders, achievers and even guests are given respect. In the West, this concept of respect is missing to a great extent. At least the intensity with which the East respects is unknown to the West. So when the Westerner comes in contact with an Easterner, he is gratified to a great extent because of the respect he is given. And after sometime he gets used to this respect. And in his mind, he might even start looking at the Easterner as somebody who is a little lower than him. This problem surfaces in many ways - like for example: Recently we witnessed it in the world of cricket. When the cricketers from Australia or England first come to India they get respect from the whole society. First, respect is an alien concept to them. But then they get used to it. When they play with Indian cricketers, the latter think of themselves and their counter parts as absolutely equal. The Westerner when he finds that this Indian cricketer is behaving with him equally, he doesn't like it. He feels, *Your whole society respects me and you have the arrogance to behave with me equally.* Then he ends up misbehaving with the Indian counter parts and then the Indian cricketer puts an allegation of racial abuse. Confucius says neither give less respect than what is due nor give more respect than what is due. Also understand the cultural context of who you are respecting and whether there is a chance of his mistaking your respectful gestures. Such prudence will make you comfortable and the hangover of having given respect will not be negative. Also the other person who deserves respects will not be shortchanged because you would have just given him his due and your relationship with him will progress smoothly.

Preparedness ensures success.
Unpreparedness spells failure.
For preparedness means two things -
one is preparation in thought and
the other is preparation through action (practise).

Confucius feels, to think before one speaks will ensure fluency. To think before one acts will ensure all difficulties get cleared away. To think before one performs his duties will ensure a strong conscience. And to think before one practices principles will ensure smoothness in practice.

So, one part of Confucian preparation is thinking - mental preparation. And the other part of his preparation is the physical part.

Bill Gates has said (sic), "I picked up a very bad habit in school and college - I started liking the Bill-Gates-studies-only-at-the-last-moment image - which people had of me. I liked this image and I nurtured it by really studying at the last moment and passing my exams and I started thinking that this approach would work in the real world also. When I joined the real world of business, I realized that this is a very expensive approach. I started failing. Then I consciously got rid of my liking for this image, changed my habit of last minute work and started focusing on long hours and long days of preparation for all major events and meetings which I had to take."

Confucius says you should be mentally prepared and you should have put in the requisite effort in practice also.

To give oneself earnestly to the duties due to man and while respecting spiritual beings, to keep aloof from them, this may be called wisdom.

Confucius suggests that we keep aloof from spiritual beings as for him the welfare of the society is more important than the sacred aspects. Confucius knew that a nation which goes too much in pursuit of the sacred, that is, religion and spirituality, often ends up in slavery. His understating has proven right, time and again. Be it the great Indian empire or the mighty empire of China or Portugal or Egypt, they all ran up to the monasteries on the hill and then downhill. In the Confucian framework, too much preoccupation with the sacred, makes the society decadent, impoverished and chaotic.

Then what is it that is of use to society?

It is doing one's duty. Confucius encourages man to positively contribute to the society and be actively involved in all the roles he plays. At home, he should be a good father to his son, a good son to his father, a good husband. And outside, he should be a good citizen, a good worker, a good boss and if he is a ruler, he should be a good ruler. Just by doing so, a person effortlessly becomes a sage, a *Rushi*, which in Chinese means involved, and worldly.

Moreover if one is successful in this world, he stands a good chance of succeeding in the other world also. Why?

Development in this world requires organization, so does spiritual development.

One who is successful in this world has developed the organizational wherewithal necessary to succeed in the spiritual realm as the skills of organizing are necessary to succeed in the spiritual world also.

Confucius also says,
A good man it is not mine to see.
Could I see a man possessed of constancy that would satisfy me.
Having not and yet affecting to have.
Empty and yet affecting to be full.
Straightened and yet effecting to be at ease.
It is difficult with such characteristics to have constancy.

Confucius likes consistency and truth. He is against hypocrisy. He feels that the spiritual man shows that he has, even though he does not have any thing. He shows that he is full but he is empty. He shows that he is at ease but he is stiff. He feels - and this has also come true time and again - at all times and everywhere, that the priests are known to promise the moon and deliver little.

Once there was a man who had a wish-fulfilling crystal. If he were to say to it, "Give me a lakh of rupees", the crystal would make a lakh of rupees materialize immediately. The man had all the money he needed and was happy with life till one day a monk came to his house. The monk wished to stay the night and the man decided to play host. Just before retiring to bed the monk surreptitiously closed the door of his room. Intrigued the host peeped from the key hole to see what the monk was up to. The monk whose back was towards him, opened his bag and took out a crystal much bigger than what the host had. He then put it on the floor in front of him and said, “Give me a coconut”. The crystal answered, “I will give you two”. The monk said, “Give me a gold plate”. The crystal said, “I will give you two”.

The host was jealous as he had a crystal which gave only what he wanted but the monk had a crystal which gave double of what was asked.

Next morning as the monk was leaving he pleaded with him to exchange his crystal with his. The monk agreed. They exchanged their crystals and the host dropped him to the railway station. In his excitement of trying the new crystal he almost sprinted back to his home. He sat down with the new crystal in front of him and said, “Give me 10 lakhs (1 million Rupees)”. The crystal replied, “I will give you twenty lakhs”. The man was thrilled and waited for the twenty lakhs but when the amount didn't appear. He said, “OK give me twenty lakhs”. The crystal replied, “I will give you forty lakhs”. The man said, “Give me forty lakhs then”.

The crystal said, “I will give you eighty lakhs”. And so on it went. To his anguish the man now knew that the monk’s crystal only says. It doesn't give.

Most monks are like that. They only say but don't give- can't give. They might also end up taking away what you already have. In fact some priests and pundits are worse than thieves. As a thief only robs you of your wealth, but a priest robs you of your soul. Then he makes you run - chasing a mirage - runs scared.

Confucius is not for spirituality. He feels, by being involved and by being worldly, you will achieve spiritual bliss.

Buddha also feels the same. In Buddha's life there is an incident when a man asked him, "Is there God?" Buddha was quiet. The man then asked him, "Is there soul?" Buddha still did not reply. Lastly the man asked, "Is there pain and sorrow?" This time Buddha answered, "Yes there is pain and sorrow and there is a way to get rid of pain and sorrow. If you wish to know, I can tell you the way."

Why did Buddha not reply the first two questions? Because he knew that by the time he would finish telling the questioner about God and Soul both he and the questioner would be dead. But if the man were taken out of pain and sorrow, he would come to a state of spiritual bliss (ananda) and then no longer would he bother to seek answers to questions like, is there God and is there Soul.

Spirituality often makes a person fearful. Also by tying up the person in cockeyed gobbledygook, spirituality makes him miss life.

Men of action, like Confucius, felt an over-emphasis on spirituality dilutes action. Their compassion for the needy makes them cry out for action. They know, through these actions, one often finds his higher self, faster. One also escapes the airy-fairy and hocus - pocus net and lands on firm spiritual ground. They know that spirituality is an important aspect of life, but one should not make it the whole of life. Else he will realize that after sometime, the heavens are also boring. Confucius believes in hands that serve, rather than lips that chant.

FORTHCOMING Books by Wisdom Village (Publications Division)

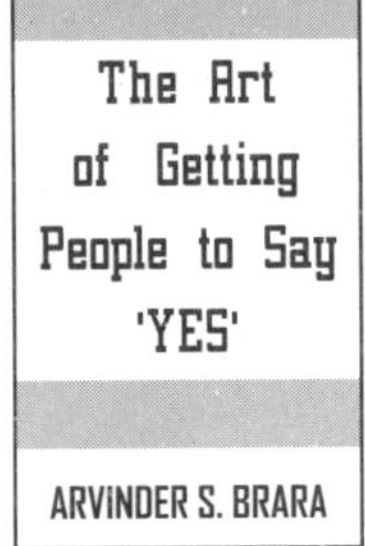

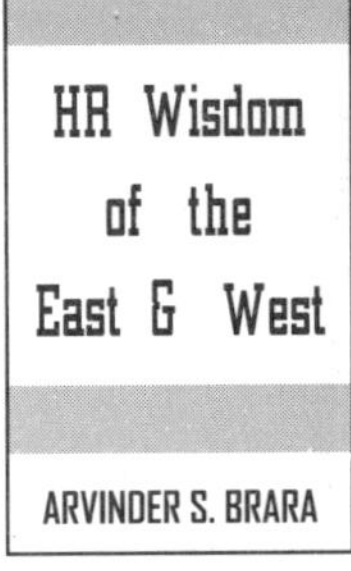

Vivekacharya School of Wisdom & Success (VSWS), the educational off-shoot of Wisdom Village is achieving new milestones in the fields of Wisdom and attitudinal training across the country and beyond. VSWS has successfully conducted workshops on **The Art of Wise Leadership, Success Management, Secrets of Success, Winning Through Wisdom & Creativity** and many more for the **University of Sydney, TiE, India Club (Australia), Singapore Management University, Bill & Melinda Gates Foundation, Tata Power, IFFCO, Max New York Life, Apollo International, European Business Group, Rotary International**... the list is endless.

Announcing Programs for Corporates / Academic / Management Institutes in 2009:

1. **WISDOM & SUCCESS IN INTERVIEWS**
   A special half day program @ the cost of a movie ticket, Rs. 200 per student (minimum requirement 200 students)
2. **GROWTH & DEVELOPMENT PROGRAM**
   A unique 5 day program, spread over 5 weekends @ the cost of Rs. 1000 per student (minimum requirement 200 students)
3. **A TRANSFORMATIONAL GROWTH & DEVELOPMENT PROGRAM**
   Especially designed for Middle & Senior Managers. To hone their political, social, material and spiritual intelligence.

For Bookings & more details please contact:

Email: wisdomvillageindia@gmail.com Phone: +91 98115.14287

SUCCESS SUTRAS FOR THE 21ST CENTURY : A TRILOGY OF WISDOM

- ☑ **Chanakya's Political Wisdom**
- ☐ **Confucius' Social Wisdom**
- ☐ **Kabir's Spiritual Wisdom**

Presenting

Chanakya's Political Wisdom

SUCCESS SUTRAS FOR THE 21ST CENTURY : A TRILOGY OF WISDOM

- ☑ **Chanakya's Political Wisdom**
- ☐ **Confucius' Social Wisdom**
- ☐ **Kabir's Spiritual Wisdom**

Presenting

Chanakya's Political Wisdom

VIVEKACHARYA PAVAN CHOUDARY
Wisdom Guru
&
Author of the world acclaimed book -
When You Are Sinking Become a Submarine

A WVPD ORIGINAL

Books from Wisdom Village (Publications Division) envision to enhance and enrich its readers with life changing experiences from the mind, body and soul genres. They strive towards holistic development.

Editorial Coordinator Charushilla Narula
Design Arpan Advertising & Marketing

First published 2009

 This book is part of the three books in the Trilogy of Wisdom by Vivekacharya Pavan Choudary.

ISBN 978-81-906555-4-5

Published by:

Wisdom Village (Publications Division)

Knowledge is information. Wisdom is transformation.

WVPD is a part of Wisdom Village
124 Satya Niketan
IInd Floor,
New Delhi - 110021
Email: wisdomvillageindia@gmail.com
Contact Person: Charushilla Narula

CONTENTS

ABOUT VIVEKACHARYA PAVAN CHOUDARY

Vivekacharya Pavan Choudary is a world icon in Success Coaching, Political thinking & Practical Spirituality. He has been acknowledged for his global contributions in the fields of Wisdom, Leadership, Management, Psychology, Creativity, State Craft & Spirituality. Today he is among the foremost thinkers of the world in breadth and depth of thinking. By sharing his ideas and insights he has contributed to the success of sportstars, film stars, CEOs and the political elite both in India and abroad. So pioneering are his thoughts that they have initiated a wave of social reform, which is gradually adding to the national fabric.

His world acclaimed book, 'When You Are Sinking Become a Submarine', expounds a new philosophy of power and success. It has crossed Indian shores and is becoming a reference text for leaders worldwide. It has already been translated in Hindi (Aisa Paal Taane ki Aandhi Urja Bane) and editions in other languages are soon to be launched.

A leader, on the path of nation building Vivekacharya has moved from strength to strength and today he is being viewed as the most promising political thinker and management speaker, shaping opinions on practically all aspects of governance, social reform and leadership. Not a pundit but a successful practitioner, Vivekacharya Pavan Choudary, is the CEO and MD of Vygon, a leading French Multinational in the field of Healthcare.

Considering his unmatched profile and the quality of his research in the fields of socio-politico-spiritual wisdom, it was only apt for WVPD to request him to compile this unique **Trilogy of Wisdom**, a path-breaking commentary on Chanakya's Political Wisdom, Confucius' Social Wisdom and Kabir's Spiritual Wisdom.

For more details on the author and to order other titles please visit www.starcoach.co.in

A NOTE FROM THE PUBLISHER

Wisdom Village (Publications Division) (WVPD) proudly presents SUCCESS SUTRAS FOR THE 21ST CENTURY: A TRILOGY OF WISDOM By VIVEKACHARYA PAVAN CHOUDARY. This is a unique rendition (in print and audio) of **Chanakya's Political Wisdom, Confucius' Social Wisdom and Kabir's Spiritual Wisdom as has never been presented before.** It is an attempt to make the wisdom of these great masters relevant to us today.

Vivekacharya Pavan Choudary, in this epic-like trilogy, accompanied with its soul-stirring audio version, provides a ready guide to achieving Political sharpness, Social order and Spiritual bliss.

CHANAKYA & VIVEKACHARYA

Vivekacharya Pavan Choudary feels for the country & its countrymen. He feels that the country should be wealthy and strong because if you are rich and weak, robbers come. He believes that each Indian should take active interest in his motherland. Like Charles de Gaulle, he feels that politics is too important an area to be left to the politicians.

It is indeed the best time to showcase the work of the Indian Machiavelli, Chanakya, for both the Indian and the Western world. Chanakya has been translated, but we found that despite the fact that Chanakya has been, by far, the best intellect the world over in Statecraft, with masterly skills in planning and diplomacy, there is no political commentary on Chanakya. Therefore, WVPD decided to request Vivekacharya Pavan Choudary (called the "New Age Chanakya" by Indus Age, Australia & other media), one of the foremost political commentators in the world today to present a true political commentary on Chanakya which will strike a chord in the mind of the politician as well as the statesman.

Chanakya's Political Wisdom is particularly relevant because in the India of today, the circumstances are very similar to what they were when Chanakya was born the country is under attack, not only externally, from extremism, aggressive neighbours and rivals in trade pursuing and pushing their agenda, but it is also under strain internally, because of its hypocrisy, factionalism, poor governance, civic norms and creaking infrastructure. At such a time, what Chanakya has said 2500 years ago, becomes relevant again. His thoughts are as valid for a common man as for a king.

Let us begin this journey by understanding this mega mind who changed the map of the Indian subcontinent.

My advice to you is to read, assimilate and then listen to assimilate more. ..let the words of the Guru reverberate and register in your senses. Drop all preconceived ideas, beliefs and be prepared to learn…to receive …to imbibe…be prepared to transform.

Charushilla Narula
wisdomvillageindia@gmail.com

INTRODUCTION

Chanakya is a peak in political consciousness, a peak in political thought. But he is not just a thinker he is a doer. Karl Marx has said *philosophers have only interpreted the world- the point however is to change it*. Hebert Spencer has said *the great point of education is not knowledge but action*. Chanakya is a man of action. Chanakya brought together several quarreling and splintered states under one umbrella. He created for the first time in recorded history a strong India, a proud India, an India which for a change was proud of its present and of its present strengths, an India which was ready to repel successfully, the never beaten armies of even Alexander.

Chanakya is as ruthless as Machiavelli- still there is a moral strand in him. This morality is his second distinguishing factor. He is a votary of guile with the wicked but he feels enduring strength comes from principles. He has stated that a debt should be paid of till the last penny and an enemy should be destroyed without a trace. In the first part of the statement you sense Chanakya's morality in the second part of the statement you feel Chanakya's ruthlessness. Chanakya's positivism is immense. He is so positive that his positivism also accommodates the negative in it. This positivism is the other distinguishing trait of Chanakya.

Political Wisdom of Chanakya

दुष्टा भार्या शठं मित्रं भृत्यश्चोत्तरदायकः।
ससर्पे च गृहे वासो मृत्युरेव न संशयः।।

An impolite servant upsets his master's mind every now and then.

In this verse the term *servant* means the subordinate and *master* means the superior. Chanakya is a great one for discipline and he goes to great lengths to ensure the right chain of command. Like Nietzsche, Chanakya does not believe in equality of men. He feels that to impose equality on a human race which is so unequal would be the biggest injustice. Very few people have in the history of mankind spoken against equality. Why? Because the egalitarian argument is a humanitarian argument, when you speak against equality then you seem as inhuman. But Chanakya differs from the world he does not go with the trend he goes with the truth. So he feels that for any organization to function, there is authority which is the sine-qua-non. A game cannot be played without an umpire. You need an umpire for the game to be played. Similarly, Chanakya feels you need authority for an organization to function.

I am reminded of a movie "The God Father". In God Father the Corleone family is having a meeting with a rival family and the rival family is going to propose to them the prospect of entering into the drugs trade. The Corleone family is headed by Don Corleone. Two of his sons, Sonny and Michael, are with him at the meeting. The Corleone family decides among themselves that they will decline this offer as they don't wish to get into drugs trade. At the meeting the offer is made by the rival family and Sonny Corleone cannot resist the temptation of telling the audience that he is interested in the deal, however, he finally defers to Don Corleone, the God Father, and does not push his point. However, the rival family smells a rat and they understand there is a rift in the Corleone family and this knowledge makes them attack the Corleone family and engage them in a very bloody war which costs the Corleone family dearly.

Certainly enough, an impolite servant upsets his master's mind every now and then. Not only does he upset his master's mind every now and then, he also weakens the enterprise as cited in the case above. Secondly, by upsetting his master's mind he does not allow the master to function peacefully. He does not allow the master to play his best game. Such servants also lose out because the master doesn't want them to accompany him to public gatherings or where he is meeting other people. This reduces the chance of social interaction which these servants get. In this way, these subordinates miss many an opportunity. They don't even know that those opportunities existed. Their master decides not to take them along because the master feels that the servant will dilute his authority or he will not be able to operate with ease because of his servant's insubordinate attitude.

अर्थाऽधीताश्च यैर्वदास्तथा शूद्रान्नभोजिनाः ।
ते द्विजाः किं करिष्यन्ति निर्विषा इव पन्नगाः ।।

Even a priest needs to inspire some awe
to command the faith of the faithful.

By priest, Chanakya means a virtuous man - a kind, honest, sincere, generous, loving man. If you wish to live like such a man your life would be saintly. If you wish to be like a saint, then Chanakya says you should have a weapon. What does he mean by a weapon? Weapon means either the ability to stand for your principles or your network of contacts and your good will or your ability to expose the other person's misdeeds. This will inspire awe. So Chanakya is trying to tell the student that even the most virtuous man needs some power, some awe to command the faithful. A western author has said that, "so that it may have a little peace even the most gentlemanly of dogs need to snarl occasionally." Chanakya conveyed this very thought through his writings 2500 years ago.

यस्मिन् रूष्टे भयं नास्ति तुष्टे नैव धनाऽऽगमः ।
निग्रहोऽनुग्रहो नास्ति स रूष्टः किं करिष्यंति ।।

One whose anger does not inspire awe
and whose pleasure gives no rewards
will be of no consequence.

Here Chanakya is speaking about how authority is linked to sanctions or to rewards. He is trying to tell the ruler that if you are angry and do not impose sanctions and do not punish, and if you are most pleased and cannot give rewards you will be of no consequence. Post Indo-China war, China encroached thousands of kilometers of our territory. Even post this encroachment, our Prime Minister Jawaharlal Nehru said that, "We forgive China for this transgression" (sic).

Next day Ram Dhari Singh Dinkar, a Hindi poet had this to say,

Shama Shobti Us Bhujang Ko, Jiske Pas Garal Ho
Vo Shama Kya Kare, Jo Dantheen, Vishheen or Saral Ho

A serpent that has venom, has teeth and has strength - when it forgives, there is grace in its forgiving, there is magnanimity. But when a serpent that has no venom and no bite, claims to forgive it sounds like hypocrisy (hiding its defeat with noble words). It means nothing and fools no one.

In other words, Dinkar was trying to tell the leadership of the country that you can only forgive when you are strong. It is in this vein that Chanakya is saying that your anger and conversely, your forgiveness are graceful only when you have strength. If you do not have strength and you get angry you might be vanquished for your bravado and if you have no strength and you say that you are forgiving some body who is more powerful than you, the world will laugh at you.

तावद् भयेषु भेतव्यं यावद्भयमनागतम् ।
आगतं तु भयं दुष्ट्वा प्रहर्तव्यमशङ्कया ।।

The wise are afraid of troubles when they appear on the horizon but when these arrive they get up and boldly face them.

Here Chanakya speaks both about caution and courage. When he says the wise are afraid of troubles when they appear on the horizon, he implies - the wise try to avoid trouble. He is also saying implicitly that the wise try to behave in a way so that they don't make enemies. They don't offend people to such an extent that these people wish to attack them. They try to behave in a way that they stay clear of controversy and clear of trouble. So here he is advocating caution. Then he says when these (troubles) arrive they get up and boldly face them. Here he is saying when trouble is at your door and there is no prophylactic which will work any more, no preventive measure which will help, you face it squarely and boldly. Chanakya is a votary of deep courage on material matters, Chanakya advises similar fortitude by saying on matters of money negotiations one must clearly state the terms. Then, the deal goes through smoothly leaving no chance for the other party to play tricks. Here Chanakya is reacting to the non-straight forward or round about approach of some countrymen. He is advising them to boldly talk about money matters, not to be shy in discussing money matters. Chanakya understands the importance of money. Chanakya also understands the hypocritical and confused Indian people who often say at the time of important negotiations ***"Whatever is mine is yours..."*** For Chanakya what is mine is mine and what is yours is yours. He is against bringing the over generous philosophical outlook of the East to the negotiating table. Chanakya says money should be discussed clearly and straight forwardly, then the deal will go through smoothly, leaving no chance for the other party to play tricks.

Elsewhere, Chanakya also says, *A man must have some achievement to account for his life. Either be a man of learning or wealth or success or a good provider to his family otherwise the life is a wasted one.* Here Chanakya is talking about one of the objectives of life and that is achievement- perhaps the most important objective of life. He says a man must have some achievement to account for his life. If he came on this earth what did he achieve. Either be a man of learning (either be a great scholar who has expanded the frontiers of knowledge) or be a man of wealth (be a wealth creator) or be a good provider to your family. Otherwise your life is a wasted one.

Why does he say that?

First of all, if you have not achieved then in the yellow leaf season of your life, that is in your old age, you feel that your life had no meaning, your life had no significance and there is a remorse which grips such people who have not achieved either learning or wealth or success nor have they been good providers to their families. If you have not been a good provider to your family then in your old age you become a burden on your family because your children cannot get rid of the thought that their parents (father) did not do enough. And in your old age because you have not provided enough for your family you are dependent on them (Most likely, when you have not provided enough for your family that means you have not provided enough for yourself also). So you are dependent on them and this leads to a resentful feeling. The children feel that you are a burden because you could not provide either materially or socially for the family and now you are burdening them, not allowing them to enjoy all the resources which they have at their disposal, which they have generated themselves and you are also in a way, eating into their time. Kahlil Gibran, in a similar vein has said that -

When the father has to share his wealth with the son, in this giving, both the father and the son are happy, but when the son has to share his wealth with the father, in this giving, both of them are unhappy (sic).

This is a very important aspect Chanakya has spoken about. As one grows old he should have contributions and he should have provided well for himself and for his family and he should maintain utility. Maintain utility, in the sense, even when he is old, he should have a network of friends through whom he can get things done for his children or for others in society. He should have a treasure of wisdom because of which the younger generation may come to him for advice. Because if his utility finishes then he will have to live a life of disdain and disrespect.

At another place, Chanakya says,

A man must remember God,
study the wealth of religions
and enjoy sex during his life.

While in the last verse Chanakya discussed **achievement,** in this verse Chanakya discusses two other goals of life - **growth** and **enjoyment.** Chanakya is not a great one either for religion or for spirituality. Chanakya somewhere knew that when a nation becomes too spiritual then it is heading towards slavery. And history has proven this again and again whether it was the mighty China or the grand India or Egypt. When these societies drove in herds to the monasteries on the hills they went downhill and were enslaved. Even in the West, for instance a progressive country like Portugal, when it became too religious it went down the precipice. However he is still talking about remembering God and studying the wealth of religions.

Why does he talk about these things?

He talks about these things because he feels that by understanding the different religions your mind expands. By remembering God your arrogance reduces, your kindness grows. These are the reasons why Chanakya speaks about studying the wealth of religions and remembering God. That means, for him these things are a means to an end, a means to grow. At the same time he also says, *enjoy sex during your life.* He wants to make society less hypocritical. India is such a society where a man and his wife would not even hold hands in public and at the same time this society has given to the world its second most populated country. We somewhere wish to be seen as people who don't have sex or at least we want to show to the world we are above sexual inclination towards each other. That is why a man and his wife will stay so far away from each other in public. In most gatherings men and women even sit separately. But this repression of the day wakes up in the night. Chanakya is against hypocrisy and so he says *Enjoy Sex*. In fact Chanakya has also said that a man who does not enjoy sex in his life is not worth the milk which his mother fed him- he has cheated on existence by not enjoying sex in life. He wants to raise the world that he lives in, to a more physical level. Remember, Chanakya is not for religion in the traditional sense. In fact he uses the religious beliefs of other states to conquer them. He uses the superstition prevailing in the rival society or the superstitious habits of the kings he is going to attack during war time. So he knows how misdirected religion and spirituality weaken a nation. He is also juxtaposing sex with religion here, to tell the society that it is as important as religion and let us not ignore it. Let us go to the physical plane also because ultimately it is the physical which dominates and which is the key factor why one nation wins and another loses. For Chanakya, everything is dependent on strength. He does not believe in words, he believes in conquest. He does not believe in salvation, he believes in preserving the independence of the state.

धनिकः श्रोत्रियो राजा नदी वैद्यस्तु पञ्चमः।
पञ्च यत्र न विद्यन्ते न तत्र दिवसं वसेत्।।

A man should not make a place his home where -
there are no prosperous people (that is no commerce to offer opportunity), no soldiers, scholars, a king, river and physicians.

Here Chanakya speaks about those factors which make a nation stable. He throws light on those traits which are necessary to allow prosperity and smooth conduct of life in a state. First, he says a man should not make a place his home where there are no prosperous people that is there is no opportunity for commerce to flower.

Why does he say this?

Chanakya understands the importance of wealth. In fact he has said that only a rich man lives. What does he mean by this? He feels that only a rich man is respected, is attended to, is listened to, can experience the pleasures of life and can help those whom he loves. So Chanakya is very aware about the importance of wealth. He knows that wealth will not buy everything but he also knows that whenever it cannot buy something it buys a substitute for that. For example wealth cannot buy love but it can buy you attention- you go to a five star hotel you will get all the attention you require. Wealth can not buy you health but it can buy you good healthcare -you can go to the best hospitals and get yourself treated. So wealth is important and Chanakya understands this importance and he frankly states it; that one of the important things you should ascertain before you make a place your home is whether there is opportunity which leads to the flowering of Commerce.

Second thing to ascertain before making a place your home is - Soldiers. Why Soldiers? Because money needs guarding. Chanakya understands that once you have money you should have the ability, the strength to protect that money otherwise dacoits will come. He also understands that whenever there has been a fight between the treasure and the tank, the tank has won. He also understands that often when nations are negotiating trade treaties with other nations in their board rooms and their interests are at cross purposes, these boardroom battles often spill over to battle grounds. That means when a mighty nation cannot give the other nation economic justice then often it steps from the board room into the battle ground and moves aggressively towards it. When a powerful nation can't be fair it tries to overpower the other nation. He understands this. So he says there should be soldiers and he is so correct in wishing for a strong army or good soldiers.

Even today you find that there are five nations in the Security Council of the United Nations. They all have one thing in common - they all have Intercontinental Ballistic Missiles. (Intercontinental ballistic missiles are missiles which fire from between 6000 to 12000 km range.)

Recently Mr. Henry Kissinger was in India and I had the opportunity of asking him that the riches of the world are coming to India but the weapons are still in the West; what will happen? He said it will be a time of tension. He said this is the first time it will be happening so it will be a time of tension and it will require a lot of resilience to preserve the wealth of the country. What is it that he was referring to? His implication was that when this imbalance happens, when the East starts becoming wealthy and the weapons are still in the West, then first the militarily powerful nations will try to stop this flow of wealth to the less powerful nations. And how will they do so? By changing the rules of commerce. *The rules of the world favour the mighty because the mighty make the rules.* So they will begin by changing the rules. They will change the rules or propose changes in the rules of globalization etc., so that they start favoring them again or start favoring them disproportionately. It is then that the less powerful nations like us will protest and that protest is good. There will be some friction and remember all polishing comes through friction. So that friction is good. However whether we will be listened to or not is the important point. Who will be listened to? In the final analysis (**and I say this only on the basis of history so far**), those nations who have Intercontinental Ballistic Missiles (or fire power to defend themselves) will be listened to - those are the nations which will get justice.

Why? Because an intercontinental ballistic missile is a deterrent force.

Militarily - Army, Navy and Air Force wise, India cannot match up to the most powerful nations. They have far more fire power than us. Intercontinental ballistic missile is the slingshot which tells them that *if you step from the boardroom into the battle ground and try to march towards us with sinister intentions, then we have this slingshot which can take your eye.* This deep understanding of human nature is making Chanakya say how important is the presence of soldiers and a strong defense for a normal and healthy state.

The third necessary requisite in a place before you make it your home is the presence of scholarly Brahmins or wise people. *Wisdom means the ability to see the true nature of things and then make choices which are true, right and lasting. It is to be informed by the sum of learning through the ages using multiple forms of intelligence reason, instinct, intuition, heart and spirit.* Wisdom balances self interest with public good. *True wisdom is grounded in past experience or* history *and yet it is able to anticipate the likely consequences in future.* This is the kind of people he is looking for who can guide the society towards the right direction, who have learned from the past and can foresee the future because of their highly developed senses.

The fourth requirement for a place to qualify as a good home is a good king. We need a good ruler; who maintains law and order and is able to protect the country; who is wise and courageous and who engages in state craft. Chanakya knew the importance of a good king because he had noticed that our kings have often been the people who betrayed the nation or public. Sometimes they betrayed the public because they wished to cheat it but more often they betrayed because they were unwise, because they were naive. In the recent past, if we were to look at our kings (leaders), many of them forgot that the most important duty of a king is to protect the country, engage in state craft and protect its people.

When *Babar* came to India, he came with eight thousand soldiers and camped outside *Rana Sanga's* Kingdom. *Rana Sanga* had a hundred thousand soldiers. *Rana Sanga* called his astrologer one day before the battle and asked him what will happen in the battle? The astrologer said, "You will be victorious Sir". *Rana Sanga* sent this message to *Babar. Babar* replied, "I would like to meet the astrologer personally. Can you send him over?" *Rana Sanga* sent his astrologer to *Babar's* camp. *Babar* asked him, "What will happen in the war tomorrow?" The astrologer said, "You will lose, Sir". *Babar* took out his sword and beheaded the astrologer, and pointing to the astrologer's dead body told his eight thousand soldiers, "A man who cannot tell his own future, how can he tell my future? Let us finish them". And this army of eight thousand people defeated our army of a hundred thousand people. Another reason why *Babar* won was that *Babar* understood that the Indian mind is a mind that has not been able to distinguish the eternal truths in a scripture from the temporal sayings. The eternal recommendation in the *Geeta* says that once in a while, when it is required, the good should stand up and snuff out the bad. In other words, you should resist evil and also be prepared to take arms to annihilate it when required. This is an eternal truth. The *Geeta* also says that the cow should be worshipped as a Goddess. This recommendation is temporal. It must have arisen from the socio-economic importance of cows in the period when the *Geeta* was written - so it should have expired when its utility was up. Babar understood that the temporal sayings which should have been discarded are also continuing as eternal truths. The Mughals invaded India as they knew that Hindus are still stuck up with the temporal recommendations of their scriptures. So they led the charge of their armies with herds of cows. They tied calves to the foreheads of their charging elephants. And the Hindu archers laid down their bows and arrows! The Mughals converted the battle grounds in to cattle grounds and laughed their way to victory. Somewhere Chanakya knew that even our kings were naive. It is not that our kings could not convince our people to give up superstitions and rituals. They themselves were superstitious and believed in hocus pocus. Here Chanakya tells us the importance of a good wise king who is discerning and discriminating.

The next requirement he mentions for a good home is a river, because a river would give you water which is life sustaining and also good harvests which keep you self sufficient in food.

Lastly, Chanakya talks about physicians. Physicians promise you good health. Physicians ensure that any outbreaks are controlled. Physicians ensure that the population stays healthy and strong and that is why Chanakya highlights the importance of physicians.

देयं भोज्यधनं सदा सुकृतिभिर्नो सञ्चितव्यं कदा
श्रीकर्णस्य जलेश्च विक्रमपतेरद्यापि कीर्तिः स्थिता।
अस्माकं मधु दानभोगरहितं नष्टं चिंरात्सञ्चितं
निर्वाणादिति पाणिपादयुगले घर्षन्त्यहो मक्षिकाः ।।

Too much honey stored attracts bears,
leading to the destructions of the honey comb;
too much money stored attracts plunderers as well.

Chanakya knows that a crude display of money cost *Kuber* his Lanka. *Kuber* (mythologically) is the God of wealth. He was also the ruler of Sri Lanka and was a very rich lord. He used to ostentatiously display his wealth and the symbols of his wealth like an aeroplane (*Pushpak Viman*) which he had and so on. All this glitter attracted *Ravana's* attention and greed. And *Ravana* robbed *Kuber* of his Lanka. He dethroned him and became the ruler himself.

Chanakya understands that an obscene display of wealth can cost you the wealth. Our society today is unfortunately making the same mistakes as we did in the past. Our industrialists, who I have great regard for, who I admire because of their enterprise, are still making grave mistakes. A two billion dollar house, a half a billion dollar marriage that is eight thousand crore rupees spent on a house, two thousand crores rupees spent on a marriage! This is an obscene display of wealth. By showing to the world that you can afford an eight thousand crore house and you can afford a two thousand crore marriage, in a poor country like India, you are not only being cruel you are also being unwise. In the past, India has been known as *Sone Ki Chidiya* (The golden Bird). Do you wish India to become a golden bird again? **No**. A bird is torn apart by other more powerful birds. This time India should become a golden eagle - no bird can dare attack the eagle. We don't wish India to be a '*Sone Ki Chidiya*' again. This time our country should become a '*Sone Ka Baaj'* (a golden eagle). The point is that we should handle our wealth more wisely. We should handle our wealth with restraint. And this is what Chanakya advises - that too much money stored attracts plunderers. He is cautioning us. And for the sustained well being of our nation we should pay heed to his words.

Moreover Chanakya says, *In hard times people quarrel.*

This is an interesting point Chanakya is making. There is an Indian saying, '*Aabhav Mein He Swabhav Nazar Aatta Hai*', which means only in adversity you discover the true nature of a person. Today the West is prosperous, so it is moral. Tomorrow if it were to lose its wealth or start losing its wealth, do you think that it will stay moral. It will start fighting hard so that it does not lose the position of advantage that it has. It can even draw its gun (Again, I am saying that this is based on the study of History so far. I am aware of and welcome a new thought current which is taking birth in Europe, which is putting justice above might & peace above power). Here again, we must learn from Chanakya and try to be a nation which is rich, sensible and strong, a nation that handles its wealth prudently, which pursues strength and which behaves sensibly.

कष्टं च खलु मूर्खत्वं कष्टं च खलु यौवनम्।
कष्टात्कष्टतरं चैव परगेहनिवासनम् ।।

*Living in another person's house and on his mercy is painful.
You lose your honor and have to always try to ingratiate him.*

Here Chanakya talks to two sets of people. Firstly, he talks to the *guest* and he says that "When you live in another person's house, especially for too long, you have to start ingratiating him, you lose your honor and you lose your respect. So don't over stay your welcome. Leave before you start becoming a burden."

The other audience his advice applies to are, *parents.* They should plan for their retirement. Have their own roof over their heads. I often come across people who say that they will build a house later in their lives - close to their retirement or post their retirement. They say that they will cross the bridge when they come to it. It is not such a bridge that they can cross it when they come to it. They have to carry the bricks and the cement with them and they should have the resources to do that otherwise they will create a big problem for themselves in the future and they will become a burden on their children. They will rob their children of their privacy and their children could rob their parents of their honor and respect.

मनसा चिन्तितं कार्यं वाचा नैव प्रकाशयेत्।
मन्त्रेण रक्षयेद् गूढं कार्ये चाऽपि नियोजयेत्।।

Do not talk about your plans
as the failure to execute these will make you the laughing stock.
The idea can get stolen;
disclosure of the plan might invite suggestions or criticisms on it
which can dampen your spirit.

Chanakya advocates discretion. He says, "Do not talk about your plans as the failure to execute these will make you the laughing stock." There is a gap between the present and your plan. The plan is usually a leap into the future. You slowly add the steps between the present and the envisioned future and that's how you execute the plan and reach where you wish to be. But if you talk about these plans prematurely, even a little delay in executing them might be seen as a failure and that might make you a laughing stock. That might reduce your social equity and your ability to get the resources - many of which you might need from your social circle.

The second reason he gives for not discussing your plans is that the idea can get stolen. Often it has happened that one person has thought of an idea and he has shared it indiscriminately with other people and one of them has run away with the idea, executed and usurped it. So by sharing information about your plans you run the risk of becoming vulnerable.

Third, disclosure of the plan might invite suggestions or criticism on it which can dampen your spirit. Disclosures of the plan might invite suggestions. This is no problem as long as you don't use them if you don't find them relevant. But if the man who has made those suggestions is very close to you and expects you to listen to him then you have unnecessarily created a problem which you now have to deal with. You don't want to earn his resentment for not heeding to his recommendation. If you had not shared the plan with him, you would not have had this problem. Disclosure of the plan can invite criticisms which can dampen your spirits. There are many people who are extremely negative and who only see the dark side of life and their criticism can deflate your spirit. That is why Chanakya advises not to speak of your plans indiscriminately.

अर्थनाशं मनस्तापं गृहे दुश्चरितानि च।
वञ्चनं चाऽमानं च मतिमान्न प्रकाशयेत्।।

Do not reveal the loss of money,
the deep wound of the heart,
the scandal of the family,
the incidence of getting cheated or insulted.

Chanakya feels that a man who loses money will lose friends and even relatives that is why he says elsewhere that money is the closest relative of man. So if you have lost money it is sad. But when you share this information with society then you compound your problem. Society will sympathize with you; at the same time it will prepare to desert you. Not only have you lost money now you have also lost the moral support or the social support which you required. So do not discuss the loss of money with others.

He says that you should also not discuss the deep wound of the heart or the incidence of getting cheated or insulted. Because by discussing the deep wound of the heart you bare yourself open. Now the listener knows what and who has hurt you. Also who has cheated you or insulted you. Tomorrow to wage a battle against your offender on an issue which is larger than your personal interest (of teaching him a lesson or getting even) will be difficult. Because the people who you have shared this idea with, might now think that you are avenging your insult and it is not a bigger interest or a bigger cause which you are working for-even if you are. Also you should not share a scandal of the family with others because if they see a rift in your family; it is grist for the gossip mills.

उद्योगे नास्ति दारिद्रयं जपतो नास्ति पातकम् ।
मौने च कलहो नास्ति नास्ति जागरिते भयम् ।।

Silence is another name for tolerance and wisdom.
Tongue is the biggest war monger.

Words are cages. Words imprison you. When you say something about yourself, after some time you realize that the definition of yourself controls you. The Swiss have a phrase for it- *painting yourself into a corner* -which means you are painting the floor and you go on painting till you are in a corner and now it is difficult to step out because the paint is wet all around you.

There is a Charlie Brown cartoon which I saw many years ago. In the first frame Charlie Brown is building a room; in the second frame he has constructed four walls around him; in the third frame he has now added the roof to the four walls. There is no door or window and he is now shouting, "Get me out of the room". So silence is wisdom. Silence allows you to live your life in a free and flowing way. Silence is also another name for tolerance. Don't think if you are silent you might be taken for granted. Silence also speaks. If your silence is of a mature variety, the other party will unmistakably hear it. Tongue is the biggest war monger. Someone has said that the art of conversation does not lie so much in saying the right thing at the right time but leaving something harsh unsaid at a tempting moment. Most of the wars happen because you have said something which was insulting or hurtful to the other and so Chanakya advises restraint and discretion.

अलिरयं नलिनीदलमध्यगः कमलिनीमकरन्दमदालसः ।
विधिवशात्परदेशमुपागतः कुटजपुष्परसं बहु मन्यते ।।

The other field may not be always green.
The black bee leaves the succulent, pure lotus &
wanders off to paddy fields to taste the honey of foreign flowers;
gets pierced by their thorns and dies.

Chanakya says the other field may not be always green. Of course he understands that the other field usually looks greener. Why is it, that the grass on the other side of the fence looks greener? Because you see the life on the other side of the field and then you compare the lives of those who are living on the other side with your life. And you find their smiles broader, their clothes shinier, and you feel that they are happier. But smiles and clothes are both plastic. Even if a person is not happy he shows that he is because otherwise he will have to accept that he is a failure and that kind of acceptance is a big blow to self esteem. So the people who are living on the other side of the fence they seem happier because they are posing as happy. And so you wish to go on the other side of the fence. Similarly, he says the black bee leaves the succulent and pure lotus and wanders off to paddy field to taste the honey of the alien flowers but it gets pierced by their thorns and dies. When the bee gets closer, it realizes, often after it is too late, that all is not well on the other side, but by then the thorn impales it.

आचारः कुलमाख्याति देशमाख्याति भाषणम् ।
सम्भ्रमः स्नेहमाख्याति वपुराख्याति भोजनम् ।।

Manners demonstrate upbringing, accent and geographical roots; and a man's size, his diet.

Lao Tzu has said, "*To see things in the seed that is genius*." In Chinese folklore there is a story of three doctors. They are brothers. The youngest brother is asked by someone that who among the three is the best doctor. He replies, "I am a surgeon. Once the disease is on full bloom I operate and try to weed out the problem surgically, so I am the worst. My elder brother is a physician so once the disease appears he treats it with medicines so he is second best. But the best is my eldest brother. Even before a disease is going to happen he administers a prophylactic or suggests life style changes. He sees a disease in its womb and he does not allow it to be born, so he is the best."

Chanakya is highlighting the importance of catching signals so that things can be understood before they become manifest. He stresses a lot on catching signals. He understands the vital importance of catching signals.

Usually it is a man's talk that reveals him. His speech to the perceptive ear is a mirror to his mind. Look for what he says, what he laughs at, and mark well when he changes a topic. With practice you will be able to construct the bridge between one topic and the other. Once you can do that you can practically read his thoughts.

It is also important to distinguish a signal from a false alarm or a superstition or else you will start reading signs when there aren't any. There has been a lot of talk about signs and signals. In India, we think that we are getting signals all the time. Even my washer man thinks that he gets signals. The other day, I heard him telling my driver, "Signals Aate Hai" (I get signals).

It is as if God has only one purpose- he has to keep on sending signals to Indians, he has to keep on manufacturing signs so that Indians can discover their destiny. And now it is no longer an Indian thing only. The Australians and the Americans have also woken up. They have also started saying that they are also getting signals. In fact, they have started writing bigger books on signals and signs than we have ever done.

It is vitally important to differentiate signals from superstition. In the movie *Troy* the defending king intuitively reads a sign as a good omen and trusting his intuition gets ready for war, makes an attack and wins. When the enemy army is getting ready to retreat and sail home the next morning, the king's ritualistic priest advises him about another good omen. The king superstitiously believes the advice because it was given by the priest, re-attacks the enemy, who was hoping to reunite with its families the next day. Pushed to the wall, the enemy fights back and crushes Troy. The ability to catch signals is indeed a gift of the universe but a greater gift is that of wisdom. Chanakya stresses on catching signals but he is very much against superstition. So when you are not sure whether it is a signal or a superstition, take refuge in wisdom. If your intuition is mute go with wisdom rather than looking for signs.

सामने शोभते प्रीतिः राज्ञि सेवा च शोभते ।
वाणिज्यं व्यवहारेषु दिव्या स्त्री शोभते गृहे ।।

Friendship between equals is best -
there is no clash of egos and respect is mutual.
They don't look odd together thus,
there are no snide remarks made about them.

There is no clash of egos and respect is mutual when friends are equal. When Chanakya uses the word equal he is referring to social and economic status. Friendship at its base implies some kind of mutuality, some kind of exchange and this exchange is balanced when the social and economic status of the two friends, is equal. That is why Chanakya says friendship between equals is best. The other reason why he says that friendship between equals is best because this pair does not look odd together. When two friends do not look odd together then there will be no snide remark made about them. The world dislikes the mighty. It tries to bring down the mighty. There is a term for this in the western society which is called *Tall Poppy Syndrome*. It describes the desire of the society to level off those who have achieved eminence socially or economically, by deriding and playing down their achievements, kind of picking holes in their legend. The society, therefore, could make snide remarks about the judgment of the more powerful, of the two friends or about his intrinsic worth being low, which is why he has to choose a friend who is much lower than him.

Society also dislikes the climber. It does not want the climber to climb. So it could even make snide remarks about the less powerful of the two friends, painting him a social climber, a social cuckoo. Thus, this unequal combination of friends is vulnerable to snide remarks from society and such remarks can also destroy the relationship.

अशक्तस्तु भवेत्साधुर्ब्रह्मचारी च निर्धनः ।
व्याधिष्ठो देवभक्तश्च वृद्धा नारी पतिव्रता ।।

A physically weak person develops a friendly nature.

Here Chanakya speaks about **hypocrisy**. Chanakya wishes of Indian society to shed its hypocrisy. Chanakya understands that hypocrisy makes India weak and non credible. He says that a physically weak person develops a friendly nature. That is when you are physically weak you pose to be friendly because that is the only behavioral option you have. You can't be aggressive when you are physically weak. You have to be friendly. So your friendliness is not worth much. **It is coming from your helplessness and not from your evolution.**

The Indian society has this expression of its hospitality which says "*Atithi Devo Bhava*" which means guest is like God! World over a guest is seen as a pest. Only in India do we proclaim, *"Atithi Devo Bhava"*. Is there any greatness really when India proclaims that *Guest is God*? Some can think that we coined this clever slogan because historically we could not stop the invading armies at our doors. Is it because we could not stop the invaders from coming in, we could not fight with them, so when they forcibly entered we ingeniously called them guests (Gods)? We have very cleverly made a greatness of our weakness. Our weakness was that we could not counter them; we could not stop the dacoits from coming in. So once they came in, we started saying "guests are Gods", even if they were actually demons. It is this hypocrisy Chanakya is against.

In the same vein, he says that a poor person may hail himself as Spartan. Because one is poor he can't afford a luxurious lifestyle so he makes a greatness about Spartan-hood.

Further Chanakya goes on to say that a sick man becomes a devotee of god. When you are sick you go to the doctor. You also go to the temple. This is because you really start feeling helpless and vulnerable. Often the greatest realizations don't happen in the temple- they happen in the hospital. Usually a man who is admitted to a hospital starts looking at life in a completely different way. He becomes mellower. The first visit to a hospital when you are admitted for a serious problem will change you in more ways than a spiritual guru can. So he says that a sick man becomes a devotee of God. It is quite natural. It is not any great spiritual leanings which are making him a devotee. It is the problem which has come to his door which he wants to take now to the divine which is making him become a devotee of God.

I am also reminded of an instance in Ramakrishna Paramhansa's life. He used to tell a devotee of *Kali,* who came to him regularly, to give up non vegetarian food. But this devotee never listened. Till one day the devotee came and said, "Sir, I have become a vegetarian. I have given up non vegetarian food." Ramakrishna Paramhansa was very happy and said, "I am glad you listened to me." The devotee said, "No Sir, my teeth have fallen". Transformation in this man had not come because of any intrinsic change, it came because he no longer had the teeth to chew non vegetarian food.

There is another anecdote I remember. It is about two friends. One of the friends had borrowed one thousand Rupees from the other. The borrower had not returned the money for many years. The borrower was also known to usually not return the money he borrowed. One day they were passing through a jungle and they saw a gang of dacoits approaching them menacingly. They knew that they will definitely be robbed. Suddenly this friend, who had borrowed one thousand Rupees, took out a thousand Rupees from his wallet and gave it to his friend saying, "Here is the money I owe you. I don't want to be in your debt". Why? Because he knew then whatever money his friend and he had will be robbed very soon. These are examples of sham, of hypocrisy. These things are only for show. Chanakya is not for show. Chanakya is for blow. He does not believe in show and so he attacks all the hypocrisies in the Indian society.

अन्तः सारविहीनानामुपदेशो न जायते।
मलयाचलसंसर्गात् न वेणुश्चन्दनायते।।

The fragrant winds coming from the sandalwood trees do not spread their aroma onto the bamboo groves, which continue to be offensive smelling.

Here Chanakya says that the evil, don't change their nature. In fact, the evil think that the good are foolish. And that is one of the reasons why they don't change their nature. The other reason why they don't change their nature could be the inertia of evil. Every style of operation, every philosophy which you believe in or practise, develops its own momentum and a counter point or a counter philosophy is not accepted easily. This is the point which Chanakya is referring to, here. He is also trying to tell that it will be difficult to change the evil people just through talks.

पत्रं नैव यदा करीरविटपे दोषो वसन्तस्य किं
नेलूकोऽप्यवलोकते यदि दिवा सूर्यस्थ किं दूषणम् ।
वर्षा नैव पतन्ति चातकमुखे मेघस्य किं दूषणं
यत्पूर्वं विधिना ललाटलिखितं तन्मार्जितुं क क्षमः ।।

If the owl can't see during the day is the sun to be blamed.

Here Chanakya states that sometimes the student may not see and appreciate what the Guru has to offer. This lack of perception and understanding on the part of the student does not make the teaching of the Guru any less relevant or less important. The truth is that the fault lies with the student. He is like the owl that can't see during the day. The light of the sun shines but he does not see it. He misses it. So it is his doing, it is his misfortune that he misses the presence and light of the Sun.

न वेत्ति यो यस्य गुणप्रकर्ष
स तं सदा निन्दति नाऽत्र चित्रम्।
यथा किराती करिकुम्भजाता
मुक्ताः परित्यज्य बिभात गुञ्जाः।।

Anyone with little knowledge and diminutive evaluation power trying to belittle a learned person is no surprise.
It's like a foolish tribal woman who ignores the pearls and adorns herself with cheap beads.

Chanakya is saying that it is not uncommon that the ignorant may belittle a learned person because of his own limitations in appreciating the learned one. He does not have the caliber to measure the learned one which is why he ends up belittling him. He equates such action with a foolish tribal woman who ignores the pearls and adorns herself with cheap beads.

A stone was taken to a vegetable market. The vegetable sellers thought that at best it can become a weight which they can use in their beam balance to weigh the vegetables. They offered ten rupees for the stone. The same stone was taken to a diamond jeweler and he offered ten hundred thousand rupees for it. It's because in the first glance, he knew that this was no ordinary stone, it was a diamond. So the price of the stone lay in the eyes of the beholder and this is what Chanakya says - that the worth of a teacher lies in the eyes of the right student.

वयसः परिणामेऽपि यः खलः खल एव सः ।
सुपक्वमपि माधुर्यं नोपयातीन्द्रवारूणम् ।।

An evil person doesn't become good even after gaining maturity, just as a bitter pumpkin does not mellow into sweetness even after becoming over ripe.

Chanakya says that people do not change their original traits if they are evil. Even after gaining maturity or growing older they will not become better. They will stay the same as they were. A Western scholar has also said something similar He says it is easier to denature plutonium but difficult to improve the nature of an evil man.

खलानां कण्टकानां च द्विविधैव प्रतिक्रिया।
उपानन्मुखभङ्गो वा दूरतो वा विसर्जनम्।।

Like in the case of thorns,
there are only two ways of dealing with evil -
Crush them under your boot or stay away from them.

The first part is self evident - when you are confronted with evil you have to crush it under your boot. *Or stay away from it* - this is an interesting area where Chanakya is trying to say that once you know that a person is evil it is better not to come in his way, better to stay away. By staying away you will not allow his thoughts to pollute your mind. Also, by staying away you will not allow his violence to reach you.

कृते प्रतिकृतं कुर्याद् हिंसने प्रतिहिंसनम् ।
तत्र दोषो न पतति दुष्टे दुष्टं समाचरेत् ।।

There is no sin in quid pro quo.
Deal with gratefulness to the grateful;
violence towards the violent
and with evil towards evil.

Here Chanakya says when staying away from evil doesn't work then do not have a moralistic stand in war. Do not go with the feeling that if you were to be violent with the violent that would be a bad Karma. When a higher life form destroys a lower life form, for the greater good, it is not immoral. Doctors destroy germs, is it immoral? No.

When once in a while you pick up your hatchet and destroy evil - it is the most moral thing to do. Also if you think that just because you are good person the world will spare you it is like thinking that because you are a vegetarian the bull will not attack you. What does the bull know? The bull will attack you - you have to handle the attack, and if the attack is sinister or comes too often, have the strength to slay the bull.

Remember, the sheep can take out as many resolutions in favour of vegetarianism but it is of no consequence till the wolf remains of a different opinion.

हस्ती अंकुशमात्रेण वाजी हस्तेन ताडयते ।
श्रृङ्गी लगुडहस्तेन खङ्गहस्तेन दुर्जनः ।।

A goad controls the elephant,
a whip controls the horse,
a stick controls cattle
but an evil person can only be controlled with a sword.

Chanakya remarks, that as is said popularly in Hindi, *"Laaton ke bhoot baato se nahin mante"* (means those who will listen to force will only listen to force, they will not listen to talks). We are very good in coming out with such profound idioms but we can't practise them. We keep on saying *"Laaton ke bhoot baato se nahin mante"* but we go on talking to them only. It is this cowardice of the Indian society which he is wishes to attack and remove. He says that an evil person can only be controlled with a sword and then he goes and controls an evil person with the sword. That's the greatness of Chanakya. He is not just a talker, he is not just a thinker, he does it.

दरिद्रता धीरतया विराजते कुवस्त्रता शुभ्रतया विराजते।
कदन्नता चोष्णतया विराजते कुरूपता शीलतया विराजते।।

Even ordinary clothes look good if kept clean.
If food is not rich and tasty, eating it hot and fresh makes it tolerable.
Similarly good character makes up for lack of good looks or beauty.

Chanakya is again in his moral mode and this is the trait which distinguishes him from the Machiavellian thinkers. He is so positive that his positivism allows space for the negative. Even when he talks about responding with wickedness to the wicked he is not saying that you become permanently wicked. He says wickedness should be just one trick in your repertoire of tricks. It is not your spirit - it is not what you are. Therefore, here he says good character makes up for lack of beauty. Chanakya says that the presence of character will make up for lack of beauty because beauty fades with time but character shines with time. Character becomes more and more wholesome. It provides food to one's relationships with others, provides nourishment to the relationships, which beauty cannot because beauty fades with time and doesn't have the nutritional value which character has.

यथा धनुसहस्रेषु वत्सो गच्छति मातरम् ।
तथा यच्च कृतं कर्म कर्तारमनुगच्छति ।।

In a horde of a thousand cows a calf unheedingly locates his mother. Similarly, the consequences of the person's actions follow him without any letup.

Chanakya says that your actions will not leave you. What he means is that you are not punished *for* your sins but you are punished *by* your sins. This is because the thought of your sins - the hang over of your sins - the fear that consequences will come, stays with you. And that is how you are punished by your sins. It is by thinking about those sins you continue to get punished. It is no divine intervention which is required; the consequences are interwoven with the act.

छिन्नोऽपि चन्दनतरूर्न जहाति गन्धं
वृद्धोऽपि वारणपतिर्न जहाति लीलाम्।
यन्त्रार्पितो मधुरतां न जहाति चेक्षुः
क्षीणोऽपि न त्यजति शीलगुणान् कुलीनः ।।

Sandalwood doesn't lose its fragrance
even when cut into pieces.
Similarly, a man of character does not lose his class
even when in poverty.

Chanakya says that character, even when impoverished or in a state of want, does not lose its grace. Real character is tested by adversity. Adversity makes it blossom, adversity makes it more fragrant.

क: काल: कानि मित्राणि को देश: कौ व्ययाऽऽगमौ।
कश्चाऽहं का च मे शक्तिरिति चिन्त्यं मुहुर्मुहुः।।

How is time treating me?
How many true friends have I made?
How's the place where I live?
How much do I earn and how much I spend?
Who am I and what am I capable of?

Chanakya wants that we should ask ourselves these five wise questions:

How is time treating me? How many true friends have I made? Chanakya understands the importance of true friends.

How's the place where I live? The place where you live should have all the traits which a good place should have (as mentioned in one of the previous verses).

How much do I earn and how much do I spend? Am I saving some money or not?

Who am I and what am I capable of? That is, what my talents are and what my calling is.

These are the questions Chanakya considers wise and he prompts us to find answers to these.

प्रस्तावसदृशं वाक्यं प्रभावसदृशं प्रियम् ।
आत्मशक्तिसमं कोपं यो जानाति स पण्डितः ।।

A wise man is one -
who knows how to talk according to the situation,
speaks in a manner befitting his fame & grace
and shows anger according to his power to handle the consequences.

A wise man is one who knows how to talk according to the situation. He knows when to talk and when to be quiet. When to be the anvil and when to be the hammer. Through his speech, he knows how to address a particular situation and what to ignore. He speaks in a manner befitting his fame and grace. He does not speak frivolously nor does he speak very officiously, he speaks in a manner which befits his fame and grace. Chanakya is speaking about speech and not just well articulated speech, but dignified and balanced speech. A social scientist by the name of Bernstein has done research on speech and he came out with a very interesting finding that there are two kinds of codes which are used by people in their speech. The first is the *restricted code.* It is a code used by people who are not rich or who are not powerful. And the second code is called the *elaborate code* which is used by people who are powerful and who are rich. What is the difference between these two codes? Restricted code is frivolous and it is not precise and concise. Elaborate code of language on the other hand is precise and concise; it is not frivolous. It has gravity. Chanakya suggests that a wise man's speech should have that gravity. Moreover, he should show anger according to his power to handle the consequences. He should not over state his threat that is, he should not give a threat which he can not execute. Because if he gives a threat which he cannot execute and does not execute it, then tomorrow his threat will lose credibility. His threats won't matter. Also, if he gives a threat which he cannot execute, which is far beyond his capabilities and which is a very serious threat then the other party might use its most potent weapon to attack him, so that he is incapacitated even before he executes his threat. Therefore, Chanakya says that a person should show anger according to his power to handle the consequences.

Once a girl studying in a University was teased by a bully. Her brother went to a good, powerful influential student to complain about the bully's misbehavior. This powerful student decided to intervene and went along with the brother of the girl to the cafeteria where the bully was sitting. He told the bully nicely and firmly, “You have eve teased this man's sister and this is not done”. The bully was apologetic and he said, “It would never happen again and I am really sorry about the incident”.

The brother of the girl seeing this change in the bully's demeanor could not control his own aggression and said, “Yes, next time it should not happen, otherwise the consequences would be dire.” The bully menacingly drew out his big knife and told his influential friend, “Because you have intervened, I have apologized. If this little flunkey tries to threaten me I will cut him into pieces right here”. What had happened? The brother of the girl did not realize that the bully was deferring to the authority of his influential friend. The moment he tried to lead the attack, it back fired. It was a case of not knowing your position and giving a threat. This is what Chanakya warns you against.

मूर्खाणां पण्डिता द्वेष्या अधनानां महाधनाः।
वाराऽऽङ्गनाः कुलस्त्रीणां सुभगानां च दुर्भगाः।।

When the pygmy sees the tall man,
he at once realizes his shortcoming and starts hating the tall man.

In this verse, Chanakya talks about how jealousy takes birth. As long as the pygmy has not seen the tall man he does not know that there is anything wrong with him. It is only when he spots the tall man he compares and contrasts and becomes jealous of the tall man. Why does he compare and contrast? Where does this spirit to compare come from? It comes from our childhood. When we are about, let us say, twelve month old and we have not started walking yet and the neighbor's child has started walking and he is only eight months old, our parents start pushing us. They goad us to learn walking quickly. Unknowingly, they plant the seed of competition in us. Slowly, because of such instances, this seed takes such deep roots that whenever we find a person who is different from us we start becoming jealous. There are two kinds of jealousies. One jealousy is the type that Chanakya speaks of here - that is black jealousy. Black jealousy is when you look at a person who is different or better than you and start hating him and trying to sabotage his achievements or try to play down his achievement. Chanakya is talking about black jealousy and telling us how it is born. There is another kind of jealousy which is called White jealousy - where you are so inspired by the person who is doing better that you try to emulate him - you try to imbibe his values, his thought process, and his enterprise and try to achieve more than him.

राजामनु वरतन्ते यथा राजा तथा प्रजाः ।।

The public follows the king.
If the king (government) is good, the public will be / become good.

The meaning of this verse follows from an understanding of how Chanakya defines a king's duty. Chanakya defines the king's duty as ensuring the welfare of his people. Chanakya felt that war should not be waged to destroy other nations nor should war be waged to settle previous grievances. War, when resorted to, should be a means to improve the state of your people. Chanakya also knew that whenever there is an incompetent and dishonest Government it blames the public. It says for e.g. that *a public gets the government it deserves*. How right he proved in times to come. When Britain conquered so many countries of the world, in every country whenever there were protests against their mis-rule the British rulers said *a public gets the government it deserves,* thus washing their hands from the responsibility of being a good government. Such rationalizations allowed them to juice all these countries and send their wealth to Britain. About three hundred years back, more then fifty percent of the total share of world trade was coming from India and China and by the time the British left India this share had come to around two percent for India. David Steingart, a noted economist has recently come out with a book, *War for Wealth,* which explains how the British held India in coma for more than two hundred years so that they could drain its wealth. So all this wealth was sucked away by Britain and all the time we, like other colonies were told, that a public gets only the government it deserves. But this was not the British Government's rhetoric in Britain. In Britain it behaved very responsibly and led the public to great heights by setting a good agenda and creating opportunities for the people. The British Government even gave its convicts, its prisoners, its criminals a chance in Australia. It sent them there and gave them an opportunity to establish an empire. It also helped these convicts en-cash opportunity in Australia. So elsewhere it was saying that the public sets the agenda but, in Britain, it was responsibly setting the agenda and the direction.

Unfortunately post independence when our politicians took over the reins of the nation they kept on repeating the dialogue they had learnt from the British, "A public gets the Government it deserves," and went on sucking the country. They were so naive that they didn't even realize that the script writer of this dialogue was a foreign invader and post independence it was the sons of the soil who were ruling the country.

Chanakya is close to the truth when he says, "The king will and should set the agenda". The public follows the king's lead. The King is the game setter. He carves the destiny of the nation. It is his responsibility that good governance prevails, that there is opportunity for all to engage in productive activities, that the nation's interest is protected in the international comity of nations and the nation stays strong to handle all external and internal threats. These are the responsibilities he bears and there is no running away from them.

FORTHCOMING Books by Wisdom Village (Publications Division)

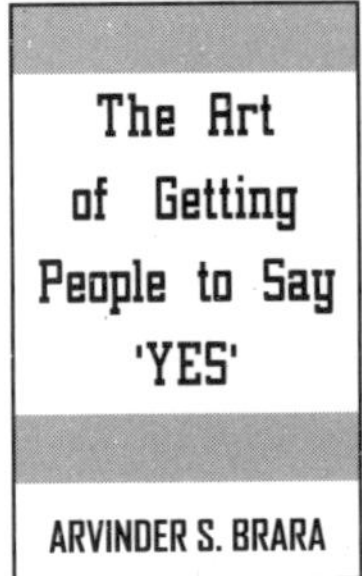

HR Wisdom

of the

East & West

ARVINDER S. BRARA

Vivekacharya School of Wisdom & Success (VSWS), the educational off-shoot of Wisdom Village is achieving new milestones in the fields of Wisdom and attitudinal training across the country and beyond. VSWS has successfully conducted workshops on **The Art of Wise Leadership, Success Management, Secrets of Success, Winning Through Wisdom & Creativity** and many more for the **University of Sydney, TiE, India Club (Australia), Singapore Management University, Bill & Melinda Gates Foundation, Tata Power, IFFCO, Max New York Life, Apollo International, European Business Group, Rotary International**... the list is endless.

Announcing Programs for Corporates / Academic / Management Institutes in 2009:

1. **WISDOM & SUCCESS IN INTERVIEWS**
   A special half day program @ the cost of a movie ticket, Rs. 200 per student (minimum requirement 200 students)
2. **GROWTH & DEVELOPMENT PROGRAM**
   A unique 5 day program, spread over 5 weekends @ the cost of Rs. 1000 per student (minimum requirement 200 students)
3. **A TRANSFORMATIONAL GROWTH & DEVELOPMENT PROGRAM**
   Especially designed for Middle & Senior Managers. To hone their political, social, material and spiritual intelligence.

For Bookings & more details please contact:

Email: wisdomvillageindia@gmail.com

Phone: +91 98115.14287

Recent Creations by the Wisdom Village fraternity

Books by Uday Sahay (IPS) (Governing Body Member, Wisdom Village)

Making News
Media in Contemporary India

Pub: Oxford University Press

Delhi: India in One City

Pub: Academic Foundation